D1356277

EDITING AND DESIGN I

Newsman's English

EDITING AND DESIGN

Harold Evans

Editor, *The Sunday Times*, London

EDITING AND DESIGN
A Five-volume Manual of English, Typography and Layout

Book One
Newsman's English

Published under the auspices of the
National Council for the Training of Journalists

HEINEMANN : LONDON

William Heinemann Ltd
15 Queen St, Mayfair, London W1X 8BE

LONDON   MELBOURNE   TORONTO
JOHANNESBURG   AUCKLAND

© Harold Evans 1972
First published 1972
434 90550 X

Filmset by Keyspools Ltd, Golborne, Lancs
Printed and bound by C. Tinling & Co. Ltd,
Liverpool and Prescot

To my mother and father

Forewords

This book is unique: having studied Book One of the series (see Strike out Meaningless Modifiers in Chapter 3) the word is chosen with circumspection. It is a manual of journalism written by the editor of a supremely successful national newspaper who is only now reaching the height of his powers. And this is but the first of five volumes. Manifestly, he is a living denial of the saying: 'Those who can, do: those who can't, teach'.

Why is Harold Evans so deeply involved in his craft? Firstly, I believe, because he is dedicated. Secondly, and more important, because he believes we cannot have healthy democracy without efficient and honest newspapers. He understands the purpose of journalism.

Newspaper men and women do not need merely to possess integrity and technical skills. They need, also, to be concerned about society. The book is addressed to 'the deskman', a universal term for the sub-editor, the production man, the re-write man (and 'man' today includes 'woman'). But Harold Evans's belief applies to all journalists—that 'the man who is bored by current people and politics will never make a successful deskman'.

The books will appeal to the experienced journalist as well as to the inexperienced. Harold Evans believes that the principles of communication can be passed on and that the sooner we start arguing about those principles the better. I endorse that view.

And he sees this as a necessity not just in Britain but in all countries where the press has won or is struggling for freedom or for survival. He has tried, successfully, to produce a book as useful to the journalist who works for a popular tabloid as to one who works for an elite paper of record, as inspiring to the African or Indian journalist as it is to the American.

When I went into newspapers at the age of fourteen there was a belief that journalism could not be taught. It could only be acquired—largely by osmosis—inside the newspaper office, its adjacent bar, and the Press Club. These experiences were and remain invaluable, but they need in

. this more exacting era to be supplemented. Formal training programmes are now a healthy requirement.

Harold Evans is concerned in this book to show how a newspaper story should be told so that it reads swiftly, logically, vividly, economically. He is concerned about style, accuracy, impact. What he says is as useful to the writer as it is to the deskman. I enjoyed particularly his assault on the source-obsessed, chronology-conscious, overloaded 'intro'.

Of course, one has a sneaking hope that perfect journalistic practice will never be quite achieved. It would ruin the favourite holiday beach-game of all journalists, which is to pick up an undeveloped newspaper and mentally sub it, re-write the intros and re-jig the make-up.

HUGH CUDLIPP

The National Council for the Training of Journalists asked Harold Evans to write a book on sub-editing seven years ago. It has been a long wait but very well worth it, and we have got much more than we expected.

I know of no other publication about newspaperwork which is so comprehensive, so informative, and such a pleasure to read. It will make newspapermen think much more deeply about their job than most of them have ever done, and help them to do that job much more efficiently.

The book is not just a recitation of existing practices, with a few do's and don'ts, but a definitive study of the whole business of newspaper production from the original copy to the design of the finished product. Contemporary methods in both America and Britain are examined and discussed, principles are extracted, and valuable practical guidance given.

Editing and Design is a unique and much-needed contribution to the literature about newspapers and newspaperwork. If its lessons are learned by journalists we shall serve society much more efficiently —to the benefit of us all.

ALEC NEWMAN, *Director*
National Council for the Training of Journalists

Author's Preface

Anyone who attempts to impose on the public five volumes at one go had better explain himself. This book is the first of the five which form a series on editing and design, hopefully intended for news and magazine men of different countries and experience. The series did begin as one book. In 1961, after several visits to Asia to teach at the first working seminars organised by the International Press Institute, I produced a small book of instruction in text editing and design for Asian newspapermen, called *The Active Newsroom*. The National Council for the Training of Journalists in Britain asked me to produce a British version. I started collecting material while I was Editor of *The Northern Echo*, in the Westminster Press Group, and I went on collecting on visits to newspapers abroad, especially in the United States where I was at one time engaged as a consultant to The Gannett Newspapers on leave of absence from the Westminster Press.

What happened in newspaper offices in America and elsewhere interested me because I thought that anything advocated as a principle in a textbook should survive inspection at the cultural frontiers. Journalism has enough shibboleths. I confirmed, of course, what anyone might have guessed, that many of the problems and prejudices of newspaper work are the same in the United States as in Britain, but also that what was custom in one place was contraband in another. From this there developed the idea that 'the book' should try to elaborate principles of editing and design that could be commended internationally.

That is too ambitious an objective to hope for more than partial success, but it is one of the two reasons why there are five books instead of one. An uncritical description of present practice would be shorter. In the length of five books one can hope to examine some of the assumptions of the established practitioners as well as give practical guidance to the relatively inexperienced. Each book, I hope, can stand on its own, though the five are meant to be taken together. There is a common theme, the conviction that everything we do in editing and design should be capable of rational justification, that in Green Bay, Wisconsin, and Harrow, Middlesex, we begin with a message and a reader, and that editing and design fail if they do not connect the two as directly and efficiently as an electrical circuit.

The other reason why there are five books is that there is a lot more to newspaper work than I realised. I learned a great deal myself as I went on; most of the years, it seems, were an exploration of my own ignorance from which I was periodically rescued by typographers, designers, and colleagues. I cannot acknowledge all their individual help here, but they know they have my thanks.

There are specific acknowledgments I will make in the different volumes, but for all of them I am grateful to the following: John Dodge, the former Director of the National Council for the Training of Journalists in Britain, who started me off; his successor, Alec Newman, and his patient Council who have waited seven years for a book on subbing; Paul Miller, President of Associated Press and of the Gannett Newspapers, and Vincent Jones, then Executive Editor of Gannett, who let me loose in North America; C. D. Hamilton, the chairman of Times Newspapers who, as Editor of *The Sunday Times*, gave me my first Fleet Street experience and who has, in his own right, done so much for journalist training; and Leonard Russell, associate editor of *The Sunday Times*, for his encouragement.

I have debts I can never repay to three other *Sunday Times* people: Oscar Turnill, Joan Thomas, and Edwin Taylor. Oscar Turnill, assistant editor, has applied his meticulous editorial craftsmanship to every chapter; if there is something that has escaped us, you should have seen the ones that did *not* get away, thanks to his scrutiny. Joan Thomas, secretary, has over seven years in Darlington and London, typed perhaps half a million words of manuscript on my behalf with unfailing skill and without the flicker of a frown at even the revision of the revision of the revision. Edwin Taylor, director of design, has made many perceptive suggestions—and Victor Shreeve, the series designer, has somehow managed to cope with my suggestions, too.

What I can say to my wife and children who have for so long put up with my disappearances behind a pile of newspapers on days off and at weekends, I do not know, except that I promise that weekends will be different in future.

For this volume, in addition, I must thank James Evans, legal adviser for Times Newspapers, for vetting the notes on libel and contempt.

Finally, I should make it clear that though I have been Editor of *The Sunday Times* since 1967 there are no prizes for spotting differences between what is advocated here and *The Sunday Times* itself. These are not official *Sunday Times* books. I have drawn on my experience and from talented colleagues, but to achieve a consensus would take longer than I would care to contemplate.

Highgate

HAROLD EVANS

Contents

1 The Making of a Newspaper

The news is thrown at him in huge miscellaneous masses, which, but for his labours, would kill the reader stone-dead with mental indigestion. He has to cook this mass, having first trimmed it into reasonable proportions, keeping one eye on the probable accuracy of the facts as stated, another on the law of libel, another on various other considerations which crop up from time to time, such as the law relating to elections, and yet a fourth, which must be no less vigilant than the other three, upon the clock. Sub-editors, when I meet them, seem to have only two eyes just like other people; where they keep the other two I cannot say, but I know they must have them. —EDWARD SHANKS

Enough news is arriving today at any large newspaper office to make four or five fat novels and fill the news columns many times over. This raw material of the newspaper is as diverse as the human race. There is an earth tremor in Brazil, and another kind of tremor on Wall Street; strawberries are very expensive in Covent Garden, and the arms talks in Geneva have broken down; a famous film director has died in Hollywood, somewhere in China a hundred thousand Red Guards are on the rampage, and Switzerland is debating votes for women again. The international news has been transmitted by cable and radio and telephone to the national offices of the major agencies, Reuters, Associated Press and United Press. It has been checked, rough-edited, converted into perforations on spools of paper, and reconverted into words in the newspaper's teleprinter department where at 60 to 100 words a minute on perhaps 30 teleprinters it comes chattering to one focal point: the copydesk.

The Copydesk

The newspaper's staff reporters have been busy, too, and the newspaper's correspondents, some professional and some very amateur, have been dictating on the telephone; and all that, too, comes as 'copy' to the same focal point.

This news-gathering is a prodigious if familiar achievement; so is the multiplication of the message by the rotary machines. But the selection, condensation and presentation of the flood of news, which must occur before a line of type is set or a press can turn, is barely comprehended.

It is the work of men with bewildering titles; in the larger newspapers there are as many potentates as in Old Baghdad. But essentially it is the work of the copydesk, of copyreaders in the United States, and sub-editors in many guises in Britain and elsewhere. These men, humble and exalted, work in private. Everybody knows about reporters. They have the excitement of being on the spot at banquets and world series and conventions and coronations (and they have hours of frustration, too, on false scents). But few of the public know anything about the copydesk, the creative fulcrum of the modern newspaper. When the visiting parties go round the newspaper office they are shown the big printing presses and the etching machines and perhaps the teleprinters and computer, but rarely do they see the copydesk.

When they do, the concentrated huddle of shirt-sleeved men at untidy desks conveys nothing of the responsibilities and romance of the work. These are the human sieves of the torrent of news. They make the judgments, they prepare the written word for conversion into the metal or film of mass reproduction, and they, by their choices and presentation, fashion the identity of the newspaper.

Simply in volume, this can be a stupendous task. The *New York Times* receives 2,000,000 words on an average day. It publishes 185,000. When they appear as the *New York Times*, they have been transformed from mere words on a teleprinter or a galley sheet. They have become, in that newspaper's assessment—and it is one which will move other men—the most important words in the world. They have been fished expertly from the erratic torrent, weighed, assessed, revalued in the light of later catches, and finally prepared for public display in a setting which, hopefully, will exactly reflect their significance. More than 1,800,000 words have been discarded, most rejected as complete stories, many rejected as paragraphs, some excised a word at a time. It is this process of scrutiny and then of presentation which every day creates the *New York Times* and every other newspaper, and the skills it requires are the subject of this series of books.

They are skills of editing and design. They cannot create a newspaper which does not have a flow of news, but their absence can ruin a newspaper however good the flow. Titles and mechanical procedures change from country to country; standards of judgment change from newspaper to newspaper. But the skills required are the same whether the newspaper is grounded in high politics or high farce. *Pravda* and the *New York Daily News*, the *Daily Mirror* and the *Hindu*, *Le Monde* and the *Darlington and Stockton Times*, and any other unlikely coupling of newspapers you care to imagine, are all made in the same way. They are born from a process of editorial selection, text editing and presentation. It may be well done or badly done, but done it must be. Words have to be read and assessed, types assigned, pictures selected, headlines written, news and entertainment organised in time for it to be printed and in forms that people will read.

Of course there is no universal agreement about the details of this craft of newspaper-making, or of the way the basic skills should be acquired. There are few textbooks and a lot of folklore. Some men swear by small headlines, some by big, some muddle through without thinking what they do, a few doubt the wisdom anyway of trying to understand the mystery of it all. How long does it take to learn the craft? All one's life, they say, in a slow sorcery of apprenticeship beginning before birth.

The philosophy of this series of books is different. It is that there are more universals than particulars; that there are principles of communication which can be learned and passed on, and that the sooner we start arguing about principles the better. Rather than to attempt to define them it would be easier, of course, merely to describe present practices. It is a worthwhile task but it is not enough. The superficial variety of present practice is bewildering; it invites either anarchic resignation or imitation, and neither is sufficient to sustain the modern newspaper.

The Deskman

The first task must be to define the area of the craft under discussion and the journalistic roles. Editing a newspaper is team work; men can play different bits of different roles and there is no common international term for the basic one of text editing. In the British Commonwealth the text editor is a 'sub-editor' who 'subs' copy; there may be twenty or thirty sub-editors on a newspaper. In the United States the text editor is a 'copyreader', and the same work luxuriates under other titles elsewhere. The term 'text editing' will be used in these books and the man who does it will be called a 'deskman' or 'text editor'.

The accompanying diagram shows the position of the deskman in the normal chain of production. His work begins after stories have been

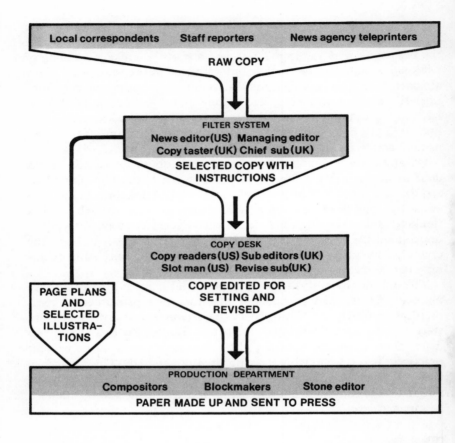

The deskman's part
in newspaper production

selected for publication, and he is then one of the manipulators of the presentation. There are minor variations here. Some offices have separate groups of men editing home and foreign news or home and business sections. American dailies often divide the editing functions between cable copy—i.e. national and foreign news from the agencies—and city copy which is produced locally and often edited at the city (i.e. local) desk by the city editor or assistant city editor.

There is an argument about whether it is better to have copy edited at such specialised desks or at a universal desk. That need not concern us here. The important thing is that in all systems the three stages of selection, presentation and detailed editing have to be organised, and all the advantages of division of labour accrue from appointing one specialist to select copy.

The Copy-taster

On a one-section paper of moderate size (say up to 24 broadsheet pages, approximately 23 in. deep by 17 in. wide), one man can select news from three agencies and staff. On a multi-sectioned newspaper, especially one with specialist sections, there may have to be specialist selectors. (There are five copydesks on the *New York Times*—foreign, national, metropolitan, sport and business.)

There is no better title for this work than the British one of 'copy-taster': the old name perfectly describes the work. He must be a man with a sensitive news palate. He savours all the news. On a big daily newspaper he will have to make a thousand snap rejections. Of course he cannot read every one of the hundreds of thousands of words that come at him. He skims the copy and because he is up to the minute with the news and in tune with the wants of his newspaper and its reader he can detect, at a taste, what is suitable. He is like the professional wine-taster. He does not have to drink the whole bottle; a tablespoonful or the mere bouquet will do to declare whether it is palatable for that particular paper at that particular moment.

The copy-taster impales what he rejects on the basic tool of the trade —a sharp metal spike. That copy is then 'dead'; it may, of course, be very much alive in another office, a sentimental pets story, say, rejected on the serious daily but lovingly rescued from the flood on the popular. The copy-taster will tell the news department when he detects a potentially good local story in a few lines of a national report. He may give out short paragraph fillers to deskmen for editing. He may do some text editing himself when it is quiet. But his basic job is preliminary selection, and what he selects is normally passed to another executive journalist, a managing editor or a chief sub-editor, or a foreign editor; let us call him a 'projection editor'.

The Projection Editor

Here is the pivot of the whole operation. It is the projection editor's job to refine the process of selection by deciding an order of priorities and expressing them with space and type and illustration. He may act alone or he may consult a galaxy of senior executives and designers, but his basic task is judicial projection. Should this story be allowed to run to a column of type on page one, or is it really a rather windy message which can be edited down to a quarter of a column? Should it be on the front page at all? Should it be discarded entirely, perhaps, so as to make a great deal of space for that picture? Which of all the possibilities tells the day's news most effectively?

On a big evening newspaper the projection editor (whatever his title) has to make such decisions at great speed. He has to be able to visualise the effect of combinations of type, half-tone and line in various permutations and sizes. There is no time to experiment. He has also to plan his pages before all the copy for them has been received. The copy-taster may just have given him, say, a follow-up of the morning paper story on another moonshot, a strong speech on pay by a trade union leader, a store fire, storms on the coast, and the appearance in court of two men accused of shooting a policeman. How much and which page and with what display? The projection editor knows that soon he will also have to decide the leading news story for the front page, in consultation with the editor. What shall it be? He knows that in ten minutes the court will begin hearing the case of the shot policeman. He cannot expect much from that for half an hour. But there are two other interesting items due to start then, according to the day's news schedule. The French President is to speak at a European conference in Brussels. There is a press conference on pay for footballers.

The projection editor has to look ahead and gauge the pressures on his precious space even before the copy-taster has received this other news via the teleprinter. Will the President say anything new? How much space should be set aside on page one? As he makes his judgments, a projection editor plans each story into a layout for each page. It is, to the outsider, a jigsaw puzzle of headline type and pictures, but to the projection editor it is a fine instrument for reflecting the worth and nature of a myriad of stories. The projection editor decides the headline type, the length of the story, and the type it will be set in. His layout is the pattern the printer will follow, but first the copy has to be processed in accordance with the projection editor's prescriptions. It has to go to the deskman.

In most offices the projection editor will give out stories to deskmen by name. In this way he can ginger up the dozy and allocate particular stories to those with any special skill or knowledge. On some newspapers the projection editor merely marks the copy and places it in a pile called a 'lift'. When a deskman has finished editing one story he comes to the lift and takes another.

The deskman is the link between the projection editor's imagination and the mechanics of printing. He converts the ideas into instructions. He must, therefore, know how the written word becomes the printed word. His instructions to the printers must be unmistakable and economical. He must not produce delay or introduce the risk of error. Where he asks for something complicated he should know how it can most simply be achieved.

This part of the work is largely 'mechanical', a set technique. The rest is largely creative. The deskman will do all or most of these things for every story:

• Write the headline which first attracts the reader's attention, and the sub-headings

• Read the story for clarity and meaning and rewrite where necessary

• Shorten the story while retaining essential facts, unity and coherence

• Combine one story with another, or perhaps combine running reports from several news agencies, a handful of correspondents and half a dozen reporters, to produce a single, intelligible report from a series of confused and even contradictory messages

• Add important background facts and provide answers for any implied questions

• Save space where verbosity creeps in (where there is *a capacity for implementation* he prefers to know *what can be done*)

• Correct the grammar

• Check for apparent errors of fact

• Check for legal errors (libel, restricted reporting, contempt of court)

• Check for taste, and

• Check for house (i.e. office) style.

The Revise Editor

Once the deskman has completed these tasks, the copy is normally passed to a third executive, the 'revise editor'. On American dailies he is a 'slot man', because he sits in the very useful slot of the horseshoe copy table facing the copyreaders on the rim. The revise editor checks the work, ensuring that every detail is correct: simple mistakes, such as a fractional error in type measure, can wreck any production scheme and make a whole page late. The revise editor also regards himself as a guinea pig for the meaning of the headline written by the deskman: does it make immediate sense, or has it grown from obscure references to some dream world inhabited by reporter or deskman?

The Stone Editor

The copy then goes to the printer, but there remains a final editorial role. In the composing room, where the pages are made up with metal type and picture blocks or with strips of film, an editorial man watches to see that all the plans mature on time. He may be called a production editor, a make-up editor or a stone sub or stone editor (a sub-editor who works 'on the stone'—a traditional term from the days when type was assembled on stone-topped composing tables). The stone editor deals with all the minor disharmonies produced by the projection editor's plans or the deskman's execution of them. If the text is too long he cuts it. If the page plan does not work he changes it. If there is late news he makes room for it. He checks the galley proofs and the page proofs. He sends the paper to press.

Standards in Editing

That is a description of the work that has to be done on every newspaper. The deskman is not a mere corrector of the press or a précis writer. There are, it is true, grades of creativity. Speed is valued more than polish on some newspapers. On a busy evening newspaper the deskman will at times find stories arriving far faster than he can edit them. There is little time for polish. He concentrates on the right length, the right news point and the headline, and then gets on to the next story. In Britain the deskman on a serious newspaper employing specialist staff writers will be expected to do less than on a popular newspaper. But all

English sub-editors are expected to do more than the American copyreader. The copyreader is more of a reader and less of an editor, and the American press suffers for that. The skills of condensation are but poorly developed in the United States and Canada. If North American reporters wrote concisely it would matter less, but they do not, and the absence of strict editing leads to wasted space and muffled meaning.

This is not just a matter of saving column-inches; on American newspapers whole columns could be saved every day and used for news, pictures, or advertising revenue. The inefficiency and waste is extraordinary. It is most glaring of all on those North American newspapers which feed the perforated news-agency tapes straight into typesetting machines. This is fine for stock prices and racing results, but disastrous for economical editing and the individuality of a newspaper; it represents a lower standard of journalism and is one of the reasons why American newspapers have lost readers to television, radio and magazines. Good newspapers are edited by the column and by the line.

Thanks probably to the effect of wartime newsprint rationing fusing with historical development, the British sub-editor is first and foremost expected to be a concise editor: to be described as a tight sub is not a sign of moral turpitude. A good sub-editor takes pride in being able to convert into half a column a report that would take a column if printed as received—and to do so without losing a single relevant fact or straining a meaning. Of course this is skilful work and it has its perils; it runs the risk of distortion when done too hurriedly or unintelligently, and can lead to the savaging of distinctive individual writing which ought really to be used wholly or not at all.

Even the most rudimentary text editing, however, is better than another all-too-common American practice of shortening agency messages merely by discarding, unread, the last two sheets. In not attempting to edit news dispatches by the word, two assumptions are made. The first is that the portion selected by length for publication is the most important—that the reporter has assembled the most important facts at the beginning of his report. The second assumption is that the portion chosen for publication is incapable of accurate condensation by a specialist in précis. These assumptions are only rarely justified; more often they are ill founded and even dangerous. The trained reporter will know, of course, that he should write economically, that he should include the most important facts at the beginning of a normal news message, and a news-agency report will have had the benefit of some rough editing at the agency's headquarters. However, several things are overlooked in this reasoning. The news agency, for instance, has the task of supplying news to a vast assortment of newspapers with varying needs and space. The fuller narrative treatment suitable for a big paper interested in the report will be wrong for another paper with less space or less interest in the subject. Secondly, there are many occasions when the best report is obtained by combining key facts from more than one source.

Concise editing is one clear area of journalism where the world can learn from the British. American schools of journalism, which have some excellences, will do their newspaper industry a service if they devote attention to the details of economical English, a subject significantly neglected in their existing textbooks. (The British, for their part, can certainly learn from the Americans how to write background into a running story.)

Command of the language is in fact the second quality required from a deskman. The first is a sense of news values. Both can be cultivated. The deskman need not be a 'writing' man. He need not be capable of a single act of imaginative prose. He should be a good judge of writing in others and he should develop a style himself, a clear, muscular and colloquial style—the new vernacular as characterised by Cyril Connolly[1], rather than the diffuse mandarin style of Addison, Johnson, Gibbon, Carlyle, Proust and Henry James (*see* pp. 16–17). He need not be a good reporter himself, and though it helps to have done some reporting, many a man has failed as a reporter but succeeded as a deskman. A young man on the *Manchester Evening News* was found painfully shy for the reporters' room; he transferred to sub-editing. As Sir William Haley he later became editor of *The Times* of London.

News values of course vary from paper to paper. The deskman should study various kinds of newspaper and their selection and treatment of news between the serious and the human interest. He should re-edit the day's *Times* as if it were the *Mirror*. He should be able to adapt himself, as a craftsman, to the standards of either. A wide general curiosity is vital, preferably backed by a broad education. The man who is bored by current people and politics will never make a successful general deskman. Of course a University degree helps, but mainly because of the intellectual discipline that lies behind it. There is no need for the non-graduate to feel out of the race, especially if he has any

---

[1] *Enemies of Promise*, by Cyril Connolly (London: Routledge and Kegan Paul, 1938; Harmondsworth: Penguin Modern Classics, 1961).

distinctive aptitude for lucidity, any passion for accuracy, any flair for design, any sense of news values, and above all, a willingness to learn.

What Makes a Good Deskman

The other qualities required in the deskman are the same as those listed a generation ago by F. J. Mansfield in his *Sub-editing* (London: Pitman, 1939). They make a formidable list, but before anyone flinches it has to be said that all deskmen are not expected to possess all these attributes to perfection. To possess some in high degree may be enough for success. Even within specialised text-editing there is room for specialisation; and a good copydesk will blend the different talents of deskmen, relying now on the capacity for quick précis by one member and now on another's ability slowly to add sparkle to the dullest text. The qualities collectively are:

- The 'human interest' qualities of sympathy, insight, breadth of view, imagination, sense of humour

- An orderly and well-balanced mind, which implies level judgment, sense of perspective and proportion

- A cool head, ability to work in an atmosphere of hurry and excitement without becoming flurried or incapable of accurate work

- Quickness of thought coupled with accuracy

- Conscientiousness, keenness and ruthlessness, rightly directed

- Judgment, based on well-informed common sense

- A capacity for absorbing fact—and fancy—and expressing them in an acceptable manner

- Adaptability—the power, whatever one's personal predilections, of seeing things from the reader's point of view

- Knowledge of the main principles of the laws of libel, contempt and copyright

- Physical fitness for a trying, sedentary life which takes its toll of nerves, sight and digestion

- The team spirit—a newspaper is one of the most striking products of co-operative enterprise and effort.

Deskmen should come to editing after reporting. The deskman who does not appreciate from his own experience the reporters' aims and difficulties and temptations to err, is invariably the worse for it. A year's reporting, if varied, can be enough. In the British training system a reporter is rightly expected in his three years' indentureship to have at least three months in the sub-editing department. On smaller weeklies where the editor himself will do the text editing, the aspirant deskman should at least ask to be given some chores (such as the TV programmes).

The ideal way to learn the craft is to sit with a senior deskman and see the way he works, and at the same time to tackle gradually more important stories. Too many men are flung in at the deep end. They learn to swim but their strokes are atrocious. A deskman should fairly soon discover his own strengths, whether he is happy in writing a straight headline and extricating the hard facts for a terse evening newspaper story when the deadline is near, or at the opposite extreme, in the slow and painstaking task of disentangling a tricky law case. The irredeemably slow man will avoid the big city evening papers (well, they will avoid him) where speed and accuracy are at a premium all day long. He may be more at home on the popular morning newspaper, where, especially on national newspapers in Britain, rewriting is habitual whenever time allows. In between are the copydesk on the provincial morning newspaper or the serious daily or Sunday or magazine.

The journalist who chooses editing as his craft will have less obvious excitement than the reporter: not for him the thrill of detection or the fast plane to Beirut. His satisfaction lies in the skills of the craft, in communicating. And there are some excitements which reporting cannot match. There are nights of big news, the late-night flash in the Cuba missile crisis, when the deskman feels he is standing at the very centre of events. There is nothing to touch the fascination of seeing the news develop second by second and projecting a piece of history.

The routine, too, has its attractions for some men. It has the attraction, unlike reporting, of offering consistently regular hours. The pay is good—in Fleet Street good sub-editors are weighed in gold—and the prospects are better. Whether a journalist sees himself essentially as a writer or production man he cannot afford to miss copydesk training if he aspires to executive work. More and more executives in Britain and America are appointed from among those staff members who know the whole process of making a newspaper: how to convert the first idea into a well-founded column of type with display in the page, from the organisation of the research to the editing and projection in print.

No change in the organisation of a newspaper will affect this. In the last few years we have seen the development of horizontal team journalism, in which a group of writers pool their investigative and writing talents and then edit and present their own copy. The Insight and Spectrum teams of the London *Sunday Times*, for instance, are responsible to the editor for every part of their work from origination to presentation and production time-keeping. But it is a complete misunderstanding of the process to imagine that this system, or any other, does away with the need for copydesk editing skills (still less the need for writing ability). The team editor will normally do this work or another member of the team may have an aptitude for it. But somebody must do it or the journalism and production both suffer. Indeed, one of the difficulties of team journalism, among its attractions, is that the team editor's tasks are so varied that he may fail to develop the specialist skills to the highest pitch. This is particularly true of condensation and production work, and when the team editor virtually ends up editing his own copy. This is never a good practice and is often downright dangerous. Everybody's copy, including the editor's, benefits from a second reading by a fresh critical mind.

Editing in the Electronic Era

The deskman will never be redundant; but he is destined to be rescued by an electronic prince from the manual handling of copy and library clippings. The computers in use for faster typesetting represent only a very elementary way in which newspapers can exploit electronic data processing equipment. Information-gathering will be transformed by the computer's ability to absorb, to store, to analyse, to interpret, to sort, to manipulate and to dispatch data with lightning speed: the computer's speed of search and of recording answers on magnetic tape is 120,000 words a minute, dealing with up to 100 simultaneous questions.

Reporters and deskmen will be able to key-punch questions from the desk and have them answered in print-outs from local and national data banks. Text editing will be done directly on a cathode ray terminal, a visual display device like a television screen but endowed with computer memory and logic. Stories will be fed directly to the computer and retrieved for display by punching a code signal given in the news schedule. When the text appears on the screen the deskman will edit it automatically with an electronic light-pencil. He will punch corrections on a keyboard and apply the pencil to the screen surface to move words, lines and paragraphs, to open up the text to make way for new copy, to make unwanted text disappear and the rest of the copy close up. When the process is complete, the deskman will press a button and the edited text will automatically be put on to a high-speed photosetting machine.

Some of these devices have already worked satisfactorily[2]. The American Newspaper Publishers Research Institute (ANPA–RI) has developed another potentially useful editing tool called Anpat (American Newspaper Publishers Abstracting Technique) in which a computer is programmed to offer news stories at requested lengths for detailed editing. 'We envision this program as a tool to the creative editor or writer and an aid in production rather than anything creative in itself', says Mr Erwin Jaffe, the Director of the Research Centre, in a letter to me.

The original story is read into memory and stored on the computer disc. As it is read in, analytical files are created for individual words and sentences or paragraphs. Counts of characters are also generated. Then, using an algorithm developed by ANPA–RI, the contents of word and paragraph files are analysed to see how important each is to the complete story being presented. When the deskman wants to read a quick précis of the whole story he can ask the computer, and less important sentences will be omitted to present the abstract specified. If the deskman decides that the story sounds interesting enough to consider publishing a fuller version, the computer will supply that, too, and ANPA–RI is working on means of enabling an editor to make whatever changes, deletions or additions he wishes in the copy. (An example of Anpat's work is given in Chapter 9.)

In layout the deskman will have dynamic graphic instruments that will enable him to carry out the kind of instant experiment prohibited now by time. He will be able to project on the screen any page design he likes, varying type founts, headline make-up and picture sizings. The visual devices will be programmed so that they will progressively transform geometrical shapes and redesign the pattern according to given parameters, such as the number of columns, the lengths of articles, the size of blocks and advertisements, and so on.

All the electronics will not replace journalism. They will enable us to make it more effective. The newspapers which are valued will not be

---

[2] For a fuller discussion see the papers presented to the International Press Institute Assembly in Geneva, June, 1967, by Dr Helmut Flohr, Roger Dubon, Alec Winwood, and Dr Robert Pole of International Business Machines.

valued for a mere recapitulation of events, useful though the written record will always remain. They will have to put news instantly in context, with its ramifications expertly explored, with its relevance to the reader in Des Moines and Darlington spelled out in vivid detail. They will have to discover more news on their own, reviving the clogging arteries of a free society. News, said Northcliffe, is what someone somewhere wants suppressing; everything else is advertising. The electronic data banks will help here because the key to information is information. And, given the abysmally low graphic quality of much of the world's press, the new techniques will be vital to rescue the authority of the printed word. In all this the deskman's skills of selection, editing and presentation will remain central to the creation of the newspaper.

2 Good English

People think I can teach them style. What stuff it is. Have something to say and say it as clearly as you can. That is the only secret of style.
—MATTHEW ARNOLD

English is a battlefield. Purists fight off invading yes-men, dropouts, hobos, killjoys, stooges, highbrows and co-eds. Vulgarians beseech them to trust the people because the people speak real good. Grammarians, shocked by sentences concluding with prepositions, construct syntactical defences up with which we will not put. Officials observe that in connection with recent disturbances there does not appear to have been a resolution of the issue. And journalists race to the colourful scene to report the dramatic new moves.

Everybody recognises that last bit as journalese. The *Shorter Oxford Dictionary* defines it as penny-a-liner's English, the inflation of sentences for the sake of linage profit. But journalists do not deserve a monopoly of odium because they contributed a word for bad English to the language. The penny-a-liner, who is disappearing anyway, is a petty corrupter of the language by comparison with Her Majesty's Government and the Pentagon. English has no greater enemy than officialese. Daily the stream of language is polluted by viscous verbiage. Meaning is clouded by vague abstraction, euphemism conceals identity, and words, words, words weigh the mind down.

The Americans are at it on a grander scale. Look what happened to 'poor' people. They became 'needy', then 'deprived', then 'underprivileged' and more lately 'disadvantaged'. A 'disadvantaged' Feiffer cartoon character summed it up that while he still doesn't have a dime he has acquired a fine vocabulary.

Journalists are daily arbiters in all this. No professor of linguistics has as much influence on the language as the deskman who edits the day's news. Words are our trade. It is not enough to get the news. We must be able to put it across. Meaning must be unmistakable, and it must also be succinct. Readers have not the time and newspapers have not the space for elaborate reiteration. This imposes decisive requirements. In protecting the reader from incomprehension and boredom, the deskman has to insist on language which is specific, emphatic and concise. Every word must be understood by the ordinary man, every sentence must be clear at one glance, and every story must say something about people. There must never be a doubt about its relevance to our daily life. There must be no abstractions.

This places newspaper English firmly in the prose camp of Dryden, Bunyan, Butler, Shaw, Somerset Maugham, Orwell, Thurber. The style to reject is the mandarin style, mentioned earlier, which is characterised by long sentences with many dependent clauses, by the use of the subjunctive and conditional, by exclamations and interjections, quotations, allusions, metaphors, long images, Latin terminology, subtlety and conceits. 'Its cardinal assumption is that neither the writer nor the reader is in a hurry, that both are in possession of a classical education and a private income', wrote Cyril Connolly.

Reporters in their gloomier moments will affirm that all text editors, whether British sub-editors or American copyreaders, are butchers. The text editor does indeed have to make many a grave decision to amputate. The details on which the writer has spent hours have abruptly to be cut off because there is no room for them. But the real skill of text editing does not lie in such drastic treatment. Anybody can lop off a story half way. Text editing is interesting only because it offers so much more scope than such simple hack work. The good text editor is a surgeon who can save facts and who can make the body of the story more vigorous and healthy. His instruments are a clear mind and a love of the language. When it is necessary to cut for length he struggles to save details by using the language more economically than the writer. He is a specialist in concise writing. When length is not a problem he edits the text for meaning, clarity and accuracy. Grammar, punctuation and spelling he will correct in his stride. The assurance of instant comprehension for the reader is what will take his time.

All types of newspaper, local, provincial and national, have to cope with copy which obscures the news, which delays the reader getting the human facts the headline has invited him to obtain. There are many reasons for this. Some copy from contacts and non-staff sources is, to be polite, only semi-professional. There are widely varying standards even among trained staff reporters. Some of the best at ferreting out facts are not pithy writers and never will be. Reporters who can write well are occasionally lured into literary embroidery. Fairly often the reporter, wanted for another assignment, is more hard-pressed for time than the text editor. And, of course, text editors frequently have to deal directly themselves with verbatim speeches sent over the teleprinters and with long extracts from official reports.

The deskman must worry about words, sentences, and the structure of stories. Much of the time is spent on the headline and the first few sentences which lure the reader; often these determine the way the story should be developed. With the constant effort to render events concrete, vivid and human, the deskman will develop an allergy to sloppy English. His pencil will twitch even as his eye skims the folios. There is not much time for reflection. The diagnosis must be immediate and the cure instantaneous.

It is with this environment in mind that the following pages suggest ways in which the deskman can improve his reactions. They attempt to analyse the fine skills of using words and sentences, and building these into various kinds of news story; and they attempt to put some of the preaching into practice. Even so they are no more than a compass in a jungle. They offer certain principles or conditions for clear expression, aware that there is no rule for original expression, that the principles may overlap or, infrequently, conflict, and that any chapter on the English word and sentence must necessarily be incomplete. It is not a grammar. Some knowledge of the pitfalls of dangling participles, pronouns and their antecedents, verbs and their subjects, and the sequence of tenses, must be assumed. As William Brewster[1] pointed out long ago, the mere avoidance of grammatical barbarisms will not result in clear writing: 'One might escape illiteracy but not necessarily confusion . . . To know what a sentence is saying is important, more important than anything else about it. That is rarely interfered with, directly, by the presence of barbarisms, and not grievously, for the most, by improprieties and solecisms, as they actually occur in writing; these things cause sorrow chiefly to the erudite or to the parvenu of style, whom they offend rather than confuse; the populace cares very little about them'.

Sentences – Limit the Ideas

A sentence is more likely to be clear if it is a short sentence communicating one thought, or a closely connected range of ideas.

[1] *Writing English Prose*, by William Brewster (New York: Henry Holt, 1913), p. 171.

There are roughly four kinds of sentence. The *simple* sentence has one subject and one predicate or statement (Eight bandits robbed a train yesterday). The *compound* sentence has two simple sentences joined by a conjunction (Eight bandits robbed a train yesterday and stole £8,000). The *complex* sentence has one principal statement and one or more subordinate statements or clauses which modify the main statement (Eight train bandits, who were foiled by a railway ganger, were still being sought by police last night). Then there is the *compound-complex* sentence where all the statements have one or more modifying statements (Eight bandits with coshes who tried to rob a train yesterday were foiled by a ganger who threw stones at them and forced them to drop £8,000).

All those sentences are clear. To attempt to say that newspapers should use only simple sentences is an absurdity. Economy as well as rhythm requires all kinds of sentence to be used. Often it is wasteful to introduce a complete subject and predicate for each idea. The subordinate clause in a complex sentence can state relations more precisely and more economically than can a string of simple sentences or compound sentences joined by *and, but, so,* etc.

And over the years we have learned to cut down loose subsidiary clauses into economical phrases. The real seduction of the simple sentence is that taken by itself it is short and it is confined to carrying one idea. The real trouble with so many compound-complex sentences is that they have to carry too many ideas.

In the example below (left), one sentence is trying to do the work of three. The first thought ends at 'future', and that is where the sentence should end. The deskman should then cross out 'and', and pick up two new sentences, as on the right:

The French Government is expected to begin bilateral talks to replace the integrated military structures in the immediate future and will be willing to exchange, say, some infra-structure facilities enjoyed by the US and the United Kingdom for continued sharing in the long range early warning system, for France's *force de frappe* could be destroyed by a sudden missile attack on her airfields.

The French Government is expected to begin bilateral talks to replace the integrated military structures in the immediate future. The French will be willing to exchange, say, some military installations used by the US and the United Kingdom for continued French sharing in the long range early warning system. This is because France's atomic strike force could be destroyed by a missile attack on her airfields.

This is immediately clearer. The length of sentences with too many ideas is not the cause of the disease; but it is often a clear symptom. It is the reason why some writers advise a limit on sentence length. Rudolf Flesch[2] urges an average of 18 words to a sentence. The Elizabethan sentence, he says, ran to 45 words and the Victorian to 29, while ours runs to 20 and less.

The lesson is that where the ideas in a sentence are complex, they cannot intelligibly be presented in subsidiary clauses separated by a mere comma. The full stop is a great help to sanity. In swift editing, this 57-word sentence from the London *Times* (left) can be made comprehensible by being split into two (right):

On east-west relations Dr Kiesinger described the remarkably non-compromising attitude of the East Germans in the reply sent in September after a delay of three months by Herr Stoph, the East German Prime Minister, who attacked the Federal Government's claims to speak for all Germans and proposed a draft treaty between 'the two German states'.	On east-west relations Dr Kiesinger described the remarkably non-compromising attitude of the East Germans in the reply sent in September after a delay of three months. Herr Stoph, the East German Prime Minister, had attacked the Federal Government's claims to speak for all Germans and proposed a draft treaty between 'the two German states'.

A long confusing sentence is often produced by creating a subsidiary clause to carry one or more ideas in advance of the main idea. This defect and others in sentence structure will be examined in more detail in the chapter on introductions, but here is a typical example from a newspaper in the North of England. Look at the difficulties on the way:

Saying that while he accepted medical evidence that asbestosis was associated with the cause of death of a Washington chemical worker, John George Watson, aged 40, of 51 Pattinson Town, the Coroner, Mr A Henderson, indicated at the inquest at Chester-le-Street last night that the final decision whether the disease caused or contributed to death would rest with the Pneumoconiosis Medical Panel.	Who is 'he'?
	Is this the name of the chemical worker, or the 'he' in the first line? We have to read on to learn that Mr Watson is not the Coroner.
	What disease? We have to refer back 43 words to the mention of asbestosis.

---

[2] *The Art of Readable Writing*, by Rudolf Flesch (New York: Harper and Bros, 1949), pp. 106–117.

The opening subsidiary clause here is 21 words long. It does not mean anything to the reader until he has read through to the end of the main clause. While he is reading the main clause, he has to refer back in his mind to the qualifying subsidiary clause. It is hard in one reading to absorb the meaning of the whole sentence.

The sentence is simply overloaded. The burden of the thought should be redistributed:

> The death of a Washington chemical worker, John George Watson, aged 40, of 51 Pattinson Town, was associated with asbestosis, said the Coroner, Mr A Henderson, at Chester-le-Street last night. But the final decision whether asbestosis caused or contributed to death would rest with the Pneumoconiosis Medical Panel.

Opening a sentence with a subsidiary clause has special difficulties for the reader when the two ideas do not march in the same direction. News values apart, the deskman should take the sentence carrying the most important thought and give it an immediate identity of its own. Another sentence should deal with the other thought:

> At the end of a rousing speech on Labour Government policies which she said were designed to remould the economic life of the country irrespective of the many difficulties involved and the grumbles of those who disliked change, the Minister of Transport, Mrs Barbara Castle, speaking at Aberystwyth yesterday, expressed her bitter disappointment that the Stratford strike had not been settled.

> The Minister of Transport, Mrs Barbara Castle, yesterday expressed her 'bitter disappointment' that the Stratford rail strike had not been solved.
>
> She said this at the end of a rousing speech at Aberystwyth defending Labour Government economic policies. . . .

Sheer wordiness was a fault in the story about Mrs Castle—but, even if the sentence had been shorter, confusion would have been created by the way the sentence structure linked separate thoughts. As Marc Rose, a *Reader's Digest* editor, once complained to the *New York Times*: 'Born in Waukegan, Ill., I get damn sick of the non-sequiturs'[3]. Obituary

[3] *Watch Your Language*, by Theodore M Bernstein (New York: Channel Press, 1958), p. 126. See also *More Language that Needs Watching*, by Theodore M Bernstein (New York: Channel Press, 1962).

notices are full of non-sequiturs, and it is no use attempting to rewrite them as single sentences, compound or complex:

A keen golfer, he leaves three children.

Leaving three children, he was a keen golfer.

He was a keen golfer and leaves three children.

He leaves three children and was a keen golfer.

He was born in Alabama and always arrived punctually at work.

The last example gives the impression that there is some connection between the Alabama birth and the punctuality. There is none. The reader has been led up the garden path. The needlessly linked sentences divert the mind to speculation. There should be two sentences, but even these can be awkward; adjoining sentences need some linking thought, as in the second rewritten example below:

He was born in Alabama. He always arrived punctually at work.

He was born in Alabama. His father came south from New York and opened a drug store with a 1,000 dollars he borrowed from a clergyman.

The essence of the matter comes back to limiting the thought a sentence has to carry. This is not something peculiar to newspaper English. There is strictly nothing grammatically wrong with the following sentence but it is incoherent because it is overcrowded with ideas:

The vague and unsettled suspicions which uncertainty had produced of what Mr. Darcy might have been doing to forward her sister's match which she had feared to encourage, as an exertion of goodness too great to be probable, and at the same time dreaded to be just, from the pain of obligation, were proved beyond their greatest extent to be true.

—JANE AUSTEN, *Pride and Prejudice*

It is hard to read this and hard to be sure what Jane Austen is saying. Is it the suspicions or the match itself which 'she had feared to encourage'? It is no solution to rewrite the passage in simple sentences. Complex sentences, provided they are clear, can make assertions about a subject more economically. The simple-sentence version that follows requires

90 words altogether and it barely copes with the thoughts:

> She had vague and unsettled suspicions. These suspicions had been produced by uncertainty. She did not know what Mr. Darcy had been doing to forward her sister's match. She feared to encourage these suspicions. She had two reasons. It was very good of Mr. Darcy to help if he was helping. She doubted if anyone could be so good. But she dreaded the idea that he might be so good. She would then have a debt to him. In the event her suspicions were proved to be true.

But a readable, clear and economical version can be produced by splitting the thoughts into four groups and dealing with these in four varied sentences:

> She had been filled by vague and unsettled suspicions about what Mr. Darcy might have been doing to forward her sister's match. She had not liked to dwell on these. Such an exertion of goodness seemed improbable, yet she had dreaded the idea that the suspicions might be just for she would then be under obligation to him. Now the suspicions were proved beyond their greatest extent to be true.

Be Active

Bewildering sentences carrying excess weight are obvious. The deskman has to be more alert to detect the deadening effect of a succession of sentences in the passive voice. Vigorous, economical writing requires a preference for sentences in the active voice.

'Police arrested Jones'—that is a sentence in the active voice. The subject (police) is the actor: the receiver of the action (Jones) is the object. We say the verb (arrested) is being used transitively because it requires an object; the verb is said to be used intransitively when it does not need an object. Look what happens to that perfectly good sentence in the active voice with a transitive verb when we write the sentence in the passive voice—when the receiver of the action becomes the subject rather than the object: 'Jones was arrested by police'. We now have five words where three told the story before.

Here is another newspaper example: 'A meeting will be held by directors next week'. That sentence in the passive voice has nine words when the active voice requires only eight: 'The directors will hold a meeting next week'. And better still: 'The directors will meet next week'.

Very often a weak sentence can be made emphatic by changing the writer's passive reliance on the 'there is' construction into a sentence employing a transitive verb in the active voice:

There were riots in several cities last night in which several shops were burned.	Rioters burned shops in several cities last night.

The active version on the right has only eight words against the fourteen on the left; and it is so much more direct, too. This is one of the beauties of the English language. Clarity, economy and vigour go hand in hand. Of course there are occasions when the passive voice must be used. Some particular word, usually a proper noun in news reports, must be made the subject of the sentence, and that may legitimately demand the passive voice. For instance: 'A rhinoceros ran over Richard M Nixon today'. That is active (and news). But it would be better in the passive voice so that Mr Nixon has precedence over the rhino: 'Richard M Nixon was run over by a rhinoceros today'.

With this proviso, sentences in the active voice should be sought by deskmen, or rather deskmen should seek sentences in the active voice. Ministers and officials and government reports are the worst perpetrators of the passive. Presumably it has something to do with collective responsibility, the notion that all decisions emanate from some central intelligence.

Official reports reek of the passive: it was felt necessary; in the circumstances it was considered inadvisable; the writer might be reminded; it should perhaps be pointed out; it cannot be denied; it will be recognised. In officialese it does not rain; precipitation is experienced. Often the passive is coupled cripplingly with the conditional tense so that, as Robert Graves and Alan Hodge once remarked, the decision is 'translated from the world of practice into a region of unfulfilled hypothesis'[4]. 'The Minister would find it difficult to agree if the facts were to be regarded in the light suggested'. Churchill said 'Give us the tools and we will finish the job'. Officialdom would prefer to phrase it: 'The task would be capable of determination were the appropriate tools to be made available to those concerned'.

These are no exaggerations. Every day in reporting the doings of government and the law newspapers let through a plethora of con-

[4] *The Reader Over Your Shoulder*, by Robert Graves and Alan Hodge (London: Jonathan Cape, 1948), p. 51; (also published London: Mayflower, 1962; Cape Paperback, 1965).

voluted passive English. Here are a few more newspaper examples, which are recast in the column on the right.

Early this morning the Automatic Telephone and Electric Company's works in Edge Lane were entered. A quantity of platinum valued at £25,000 was stolen from a safe which was burnt open. The watchman, Mr Herbert Clarke, aged 57, who is a widower residing at Albany Road, Liverpool, was coshed and tied up.	Thieves coshed the watchman and stole £25,000 worth of platinum at the Automatic Telephone and Electric Co. works in Edge Lane early today. They tied up the watchman, Mr Herbert Clarke, aged 57, and burnt open the safe. . . .
A petition requesting a reduced speed limit in Clay Road, between Jefferson and Calkin Road, was presented to the Henrietta Town Board last night.	Thirty-two householders petitioned Henrietta Town Board last night for a lower speed limit in Clay Road, between Jefferson and Calkins roads.

The second paragraph (below) of the same report illustrates the earlier point in this section on the need for simple sentences. All too frequently a sentence with one flaw is succeeded by a sentence with a different flaw: compare the involved sentence on the left with the recast version on the right.

The Board immediately turned the petition—signed by 32 home-owners—over to its public safety committee for study and possible referral to the State Traffic Commission. Home-owners are asking that the speed limit be reduced from 50 miles per hour to 35 mph.	The Board passed the petition to its public safety committee for study and possible referral to the State Traffic Commission. They want the 50 mph limit cut to 30 mph.

Be Positive

Sentences should assert. The newspaper reader above all does not want to be told what is not. He should be told what is. As a general rule, a deskman should strive to express even a negative in a positive form. In each case, the version on the right is preferable:

The project was not successful.	The project failed.
The company says it will not now proceed with the plan.	The company says it has abandoned the plan.

| Joe Bloggs, who escaped last week, has still not been caught. | Joe Bloggs . . . is still free. |
| They did not pay attention to the complaint. | They ignored the complaint. |

Sometimes the editing is more difficult. Here is a sentence which attempts to be positive, but has a negative thought intruding. The subsidiary clauses do not help:

> From a military no more than from a political point of view can the successful Vietcong attacks against United States bases in South Vietnam, which killed or wounded 134 Americans, be brushed away in cursory fashion.

This can be recast directly and clearly, though still negatively (below left); it is better still to express the thought positively (right):

| The successful Vietcong attacks against United States bases in South Vietnam, which killed or wounded 134 Americans, cannot be brushed away in cursory fashion either politically or militarily. | The successful Vietcong attacks against United States bases in South Vietnam, which killed or wounded 134 Americans, have both political and military significance. |

The double negative in particular should be avoided: 'It is unlikely that pensions will not be raised' means 'It is likely that pensions will be raised'. Negative expression is frequent in government and company reports. Here (left) is a sentence of barely comprehensible officialese. What it possibly means (we can never be sure) is on the right:

| The figures seem to us to provide no indication that costs and prices . . . would not have been lower if competition had not been restricted. | The figures seem to us to provide no indication that competition would have produced higher costs and prices. |

Such negative expressions are often a substitute for thought and decision. Newspapers which insist on positive expression run some risk of being accused of distortion; and of course accuracy is paramount, especially in direct quotation. But there are penalties, too, in accepting the needlessly negative expression: penalties in bemusing and hoodwinking the reader and debilitating the language. James Thurber, a passionate advocate of the positive statement, should have the last word:

> If a person is actually ill, the important thing is to find out not how he doesn't feel. He should state his symptoms more specifically— 'I have a gnawing pain here, that comes and goes', or something of the sort. There is always the danger, of course, that one's listeners will cut in with a long description of how *they* feel; this can usually be avoided by screaming.[5]

Avoid Monotony

The injunctions above, to prefer sentences which actively and positively express a single thought, may sound like a recipe for monotony. This would be to underestimate the possibilities of the English language. Setting a limit of around thirty words to the length of sentences does not mean that every sentence must be thirty words. Some can be as short as eight words. If an eight-word sentence is followed by a longer sentence, introduced by a short subsidiary clause, a variation in pace is apparent—as these last two sentences, I hope, suggest. Sentences may also vary in form, between simple and complex-compound; in function, between statements, commands, questions and exclamations; and in style, between loose, periodic and balanced. This is a rough distinction. It is worth acknowledging, however, because a succession of sentences of the same style produces a distinct effect of rhythm.

Loose sentences run on with fact after fact in natural conversational sequence.

> There were the translators in their booths, and the girl secretaries at their tables, and the peak-capped policemen at the doors, and the gallimaufry of the Press seething and grumbling and scribbling and making half-embarrassed jokes in its seats.

That sentence could end and make sense in a number of places. There is no climax. It rolls on. (It is also, incidentally, vivid and effective scene-setting.)

---

[5] *My Life and Hard Times*, by James Thurber (London: Hamish Hamilton, 1950), p. 150; (Harmondsworth: Penguin, 1948).

Periodic sentences, by contrast, retain the climax to the end. The grammatical structure in a true periodic sentence is not complete until the full stop.

> At 60 miles an hour the loudest noise in this new Rolls Royce comes from the electric clock.

The next sentence could end earlier, but it would also be classified as a periodic sentence:

> Liverpool Street is the finest point of departure in the whole of Southern England because wherever you go from it, whether to Southend or, ultimately, to Outer Mongolia, it cannot fail to be an improvement.

Balanced sentences are works of deliberate symmetry.

> The crisis in Cuba is a crisis of nuclear power.

> It will not be done by the law or Government; it cannot be done by Parliament.

Nobody can lay down a formula for varying sentences. It is part of the mystery of language. Sentences must respond to the thoughts being expressed. All that the deskman who cares about style can do is study the subtleties of rhythm in good authors[6] and to take to ordinary copy a few generalisations which genius, he must understand, can always upset.

The generalisations themselves are based on the idea, again vulnerable to talent, that a prolonged succession of sentences of the same style or the same form is bad. With those cautions, it can be said that a succession of simple sentences is jerky, a succession of loose sentences relaxed or even slovenly, a succession of periodic sentences formal and stiff. The periodic sentence is emphatic but a great many following one another is wearing. The reader is always in suspense, as Mark Twain remarked about the German sentence: 'Whenever the literary German dives into a sentence, that is the last you are going to see of him till he emerges on the other side of the Atlantic with his verb in his mouth'.

---

[6] Apart from the Rolls Royce advertisement, the sentences here have been taken from *Daily English*, by George Liddle and F E Pardoe, published for the National Council for the Training of Journalists, 1964. Some of the best newspaper pieces collected there are admirable for studying rhythm. See for instance (p. 95) a leader from *The Times*; (p. 55) W J Weatherby; and (p. 37) Alistair Cooke. There is also a discussion of sentence style in *Our Eanguage*, by Simeon Potter (Harmondsworth: Pelican, 1950), pp. 10–103.

A loose sentence provides relief. Brewster thought a fair proportion of periodic sentences to loose sentences to be even more formal. The reader feels he is being bullied by some arrogant swot. It sounds contrived; dammit, it is contrived. But, of course, the balanced or periodic sentence provides bite to a succession of loose sentences. Particularly monotonous is a succession of loose sentences which are compound in form with two co-ordinate clauses linked by a conjunction:

The firemen climbed their ladders and they rescued all the women. Two doctors came by ambulance and treated all the injured. The ground floor was saved but the top floor collapsed. Firemen warned the crowds while police moved them back. The hotel owner arrived and said he could say nothing.

If in doubt about the rhythm of a piece of writing, try saying it aloud. This passage comes over as a boring sing-song.

3 Words

Even without improving the structure of a sentence—often there is no time to rewrite—a deskman can rescue bad copy by caring for the words. He should prefer the short word to the long, the simple word to the complex, the concrete word to the abstract. He should prefer Anglo-Saxon words to foreign. He should suspect words with prefixes and suffixes, with syllables like *pre, re, de, anti* and *isation, ousness, ation, ality.* A deskman may sometimes dawdle but he should never indulge in procrastination. He should publish an order for the release of buses, but never for the derequisition of transportation. Honorariums per diem and per annum he should forgo, but he should accept money daily and yearly. When he sees bloody international conflict, he should make war with his pen. And at all times he should be parsimonious, not to say miserly, with words. Nothing is so tiring to the reader as excavating nuggets of meaning from mountains of words. Nothing so distinguishes good writing as vivid economy. In a line of a Shakespearean sonnet, every syllable is suggestive.

To come down to earth there is a joke about a fishmonger which makes the point. It is an old joke, but perhaps we can regard it as sanctified by custom; and say it should be recited as an initiation ceremony for text editors.

The fishmonger had a sign which said:

FRESH FISH SOLD HERE

The fishmonger had a friend who persuaded him to rub out the word FRESH—because naturally he wouldn't expect to sell fish that wasn't fresh; to rub out the word HERE—because naturally he's selling it here, in the shop; to rub out the word SOLD—because naturally he isn't giving it away; and finally to rub out the word FISH—because you can smell it a mile off.

Saving space is one imperative which concentrates the deskman's mind on saving words. It is not the most important. Words should be saved because good English is concise. In Herbert Spencer's dictum, the test of style is 'economy of the reader's attention,' and economy has never been better defined than by Strunk in his short classic work.[1]

> Vigorous writing is concise. A sentence should contain no unnecessary words, a paragraph no unnecessary sentences, for the same reason that a drawing should contain no unnecessary lines and a machine no unnecessary parts. This requires not that the writer make all his sentences short, or that he avoid all detail and treat his subjects only in outline, but that every word tell.

That is the theme of this chapter, and indeed of this book. What is said here about good English may be compared with what a later volume has to say about good design. Look after the words and style will look after itself. This does consist in part of doing what the fishmonger's friend did. Every word should be scrutinised. If it is not a working word, adding sense to a sentence, it should be struck out. There are many occasions when the mere shedding of surplus fat invigorates the sentence. At other times concise writing requires substituting one word for another word or groups of words. It is the marriage of economy and accuracy which is wanted: the right words in the right order.

Newspapers are supposed to be jealous of their space. Yet every day, by slack writing, thousands of words are wasted. It is worst on North American and Indian newspapers; it is somewhat better, but not much, on Australian newspapers; and best, but a long, long way from what it might be, in British newspapers. This wastage means the loss of many columns which could be used for news. But the central fact to grasp about the text editor is that he is not engaged simply on a space-saving exercise. Sentences carrying dross not only take up more space than they should. They obscure meaning.

Economy has to be pursued with intelligence. Indiscriminate slaughter is no virtue. Some writers build monstrous adjectival phrases in an effort to save on prepositions. It is breathless and unclear:

After a *No. 10 Downing Street call,*   Did they call him?
*Foreign Secretary Sir Alec Douglas
Home* flew last night to Tel Aviv to
seek a new *peace plan agreement.*

Modifiers help economical writing, but strung together like sausages

---

[1] *Elements of Style*, by W Strunk Jnr (New York: Macmillan, 1959).

they no longer resemble prose. Some newspapers and magazines even strike out the definite and indefinite articles. Here is a typical result of allegedly terse but unthinking editing (taken from Britain's professional press journal, *Press Gazette*).

> Publication of a supplement in the Kent Messenger Group's Evening Post to mark Rochester-based Elliott Flight Automation's third Queen's Award was followed by an invitation from the avionics firm to see Concorde production in Bristol.

And again:

> Group to help more than 80 'women in anguish'—those suffering from depression—has been launched by South East London Mercury.

> Death took place in hospital yesterday.

This style is crude and imprecise. It is sometimes done to avoid opening with 'a' or 'the' or beginning several sentences with the same article. The correct answer is to change some of the sentence structure. The definite and indefinite articles are essential to a sentence. They define the subject. Merely omitting them invites brutal ambiguity:

> He promised delivery to the chief executive and managing director.

Did he promise it to one man with two titles or to two men?

If concise writing requires more thought than that, it can be helped by fidelity to certain general principles. To call them rules would be a disservice to the flexibility of English and the ingenuity of those who write it. The principles can be 'bent' by those who know how. If a shrill note creeps into the advocacy of those principles in the following pages, this note of latitude may be summoned in relief and the dogmatism excused, I hope, as exasperation in the face of the enemy.

Use Specific Words

This means calling a spade a spade and not a factor of production. Abstract words should be chased out in favour of specific, concrete words. Sentences should be full of bricks, beds, houses, cars, cows, men and women. Detail should drive out generality. And everything should be related to human beings. The great escape should be made from 'mere intellectualism, with its universals and essences, to concrete particulars, the smell of human breath, the sound of voices, the stir of living'[2].

Deskmen should always aim to make the words bear directly on the reader. People can recognise themselves in stories about particulars. The abstract is another world. It requires an effort of imagination to transport ourselves there. The writer should bring it to us. Economic and political stories abound with abstractions which seem incapable of such translation, but it can be done if the deskmen will 'follow it out to the end of the line', in the words of Turner Catledge of the *New York Times*. At the end of the line of every seemingly abstract proposal there is a group and an individual.

A 'domestic accommodation improvement programme' comes out as Government money for people willing to spend more of their own on house repairs. The 'deterioration of the traffic situation' comes out as your wife caught in a traffic jam taking the children to school. An 'improvement in workers' facilities' comes out as a new canteen with sausage and eggs at $17\frac{1}{2}$p; the 'decreased incidence of cinemagoing' is fewer people going to the cinema; an 'inevitable amount of redundancy' is the sack for sixty-six men.

This is advice on two levels. It is about abstract words and it is about abstract stories. I recognise, of course, that there are times when the general, abstract word is a saver of space, and that there are stories which must be carried on in large part in abstractions. But in both instances the abstraction should be preceded by the particular. The abstract word should be given flesh and the abstract story should be spiced with examples. If we are invited to read about inflation we should first be aroused by a reference to prices in the shops; a report on Britain's cotton exports to Scandinavia should start with the dresses the Swedish girls are wearing. The story may have to be carried on in terms of abstractions like exports, credits and design, but the reader should be borne up by particular examples.

Official departments all over the world are great manufacturers of the abstract. So uniform is the language, so devoid of human life, that there

---

[2] C E Montague in that delightful book *A Writer's Notes on his Trade* (Harmondsworth: Pelican, 1949), p. 147.

must be an electronic device which expunges any suggestion that people in offices with document files are trying to make decisions about other people. Wherever possible, people are rendered into abstractions or even machinery. Robert Graves and Alan Hodge[3] tell a story of a junior official who once drafted a public announcement beginning, 'The Minister has decided to inaugurate a statistical section'. It was suggested to him that the appointment of one officer scarcely constituted a section. Wisely he agreed. He altered the draft to read: 'The Minister has decided to inaugurate the nucleus of a statistical section'.

There should be a reverse electronic detector in newspaper offices which changes all the abstractions back again into people. Too many of them get through into print.

The weakness of the next example (left) in an American local daily is that no reader thinks of himself as a violator. In the rewritten version (right) the first three words tell the reader that this might be about him:

Fines up to $50 and imprisonment up to 30 days could be placed against a violator if a mandatory sprinkling ban has to be imposed by the County Water Authority.

Sprinkling your lawn could put you in jail for 30 days or cost you a $50 fine if the Water Authority has to ban it.

And here is another American example:

The Blue Cross insurance director said that data represents the first instance in which utilisation experience of a large prepayment carrier in covering in-patient mental illness has been analysed.

This probably means that the figures give the first chance to see what happens when people are invited to insure heavily against going into mental hospital.

Often it is hard to know what the official language means. A negative decision is wrapped up as a positive:

The non-compensable evaluation heretofore assigned certain veterans for their service-connected disability is confirmed and continued.

That meant that veterans whose physical condition had not changed would not get any money.

---

[3] *The Reader Over Your Shoulder* (London: Jonathan Cape, 1948), p. 53.

Writing with specific words is generally shorter as well as more interesting. A letter-writer to *The Times* once told[4] how he asked a Government department for a book and had been 'authorised to acquire the work in question by purchase through the ordinary trade channels', i.e. buy it. On the left is an example of abstraction in a letter to myself; the rewritten version on the right saves 62 words.

We are all aware of the significant need to maintain uppermost in the mind of mankind the stark need of avoiding bloody international conflict. One method by which this can be nurtured is to revive the solemn aspect of the great loss of life which has resulted from such catastrophic struggles, within the theatres of war. The attachment is associated with such an endeavour . . . I would appreciate a directive to your staff to review the attachment for the purpose of orienting this information so as to evolve a reasonably newsworthy article through your newspaper toward the end stated above.	Men need reminding of the horrors of war. One way to do it is to honour those who died and I would appreciate it if you could use the attached information for a report on our ideas.

The advice to use specific language is not a trick of journalism. All great writing focuses our minds on the significant details of human life. Compare Herbert Spencer's concoction in the left-hand column with the original language of literature:

In proportion as the manners, customs, and amusements of a nation are cruel and barbarous, the regulations of their penal code will be severe.	In proportion as men delight in battles, bull fights and combats of gladiators, will they punish by hanging, burning and the rack.

Nelson's signal, 'England expects that every man will do his duty', lives on. Neither the sentence nor the English fleet would have survived if he had signalled 'It is the national expectation that all serving personnel will complete their tasks to satisfaction'.

[4] Quoted in *Usage and Abusage,* by Eric Partridge (London: Hamish Hamilton, 1954), p. 121; (also published Harmondsworth: Penguin, 1963).

Fowler would have identified that as periphrasis—putting things in a roundabout way. Other people say pleonasm, which is an awkward Greek word, or diffuseness, verbiage, circumlocution, padding, or just plain wordiness. Whatever the disease, it can be checked early on because it so quickly exhibits as a symptom abstract nouns such as

> amenities, activities, operation, purpose, condition, case, character, facilities, circumstances, nature, disposition, proposition, purposes, situation, description, issue, indication, regard, reference, respect, death, connection, instance, eventuality, neighbourhood.

In advanced cases there are strings of such nouns depending on one another and on compound prepositions such as in favour of, the purposes of, in connection with, with reference to, with a view to.

Here (right) is Fowler's translation of just such a statement:

The accident was caused through the dangerous *nature* of the spot, the hidden *character* of the side road and the utter *absence* of any warning or danger signal.	The accident happened because the spot was dangerous, the side road hidden and no warning.

Newspapers are full of such irritants as the left-hand version. An article in the *Financial Times*, picked up at random, writes about natural gas with this succession of phrases:

> Strategic question, the central issue, the open question, the size of the problem, the circumstances, certain questions, the most troublesome issue, the question of storage, the problem, the major decision, its immediate problem, far more real an issue is the question, further development, the position, energy picture, a question of policy, overall development, problems of achieving coordination . . .

It rounds off with: 'The issue is so far off that for the moment it remains something of a red herring'.

What follows now is a list of other newspaper examples. Each time a writer is about to use these abstractions, or a deskman to pass them, each should ask himself what the words stand for. Words stand for ideas, objects and feelings. Vagueness comes from the failure to marry word to idea. What is 'an issue', what is 'development', what are 'facilities'?

Accommodation

The theatre has seating accommodation for 600.	The theatre seats 600.
More people than the hall could accommodate were crowded into . . .	An impossibility. Again it probably means seat.

Activity

They enjoyed recreational activity.	They liked games.
The King agreed to limited exploration activity.	The King agreed to limited exploration.

Basis

He agreed to play on an amateur basis.	He agreed to play as an amateur.
They accepted employment on a part-time basis.	They accepted part-time work.

Conditions/Character

The Irish were forced to live in slum conditions.	The Irish were forced to live in slums.
The Argentine delegate said the claims were of a far-reaching character.	The Argentine delegate said the claims were far-reaching.
The survivors were in a desperate condition.	The survivors were desperate.
Warmer conditions will prevail.	It will be warmer.
Adverse climatic conditions.	Bad weather.

Facilities/Amenities

Shopping facilities/amenities.	Shops.
Car parking facilities/amenities.	Car park(s).
Ablution facilities/amenities.	Wash-basins (rooms).

Fact that

In spite of the fact that . . . due to the fact that . . . because of the fact that . . . on account of the fact that.

Although; since; or because.

Field

A further vital field in which Government policy is strangling initiative is the export field.

Government policy is also strangling exporters' initiative.

Those invading barbarians, *issue* and *problem*, often in league with *the question*, run through newspapers everywhere, stealing space and laying waste to living images. This is one of the places where adjectives can be called to duty. The verb, too, can put the invaders to rout.

Issue/problem

Another *issue* concerning the governors is *the problem* of lateness which has been increasing among the sixth form.

The governors are also worried by increasing lateness among sixth-formers.

On the *troublesome issue* of school meals, the council decided to delay a decision until April.

The council put off the troublesome school-meals decision until April.

Far more real *an issue* in the long term is *the question* of what happens if further gas discoveries are made in the old or new concessions or what happens if they are not. *The position* will become clearer in several years' time when further exploration is done. Then the Gas Council must decide what to do with any further reserves and how fast it should deplete its present resources. More gas and/or faster depletion of existing gas would greatly change the energy picture in Britain. Gas would flow to the bulk markets, displacing coal as well as oil. Price would again become *a question of* policy, as would the possibilities of electricity generation.

What if more gas were found in the next few years? The Gas Council would have to decide on a rate of use, for gas could flow to the bulk market, displacing coal as well as oil. The arguments on price, and about using gas to make electricity, would be re-opened.

Operations

Building operations.

Operations is quite unnecessary. Building/mining is enough.

Participation

The tenants were seeking participation in the making of price policy.

The tenants wanted to help decide the rents.

Position

The Prime Minister said the sanctions position will then be reviewed.

The Prime Minister said sanctions will then be reviewed.

Proposition

Inflationary land costs had made it a completely uneconomic proposition to rebuild.

Rising land prices had made it too costly to rebuild.

Purposes

Land for development purposes.

Land for building.

An instrument for surgical purposes.

A surgical instrument.

A committee for administrative purposes.

A committee to run it.

Question

Over the question of supply, the major decision in the near future will be that of a third terminal.

The major supply decision in the near future will be on building a third terminal.

Situation

The teacher supply situation is serious.

Teachers are scarce.

An emergency meeting will be called to discuss the situation whereby 900 tins of suspect corned beef were accidentally distributed.

An emergency meeting will discuss how 900 tins of suspect corned beef were accidentally sold.

Use of

The Citizens Committee said the use of buses should be stepped up.	The Citizens Committee said more buses should be used.
The use of 37 gardens has been volunteered by their owners.	Thirty-seven residents have offered gardens.

Here is an extract which combines several examples in one paragraph.

Because of severe drought conditions, the Dansville water supply has reached a critical state. Rolland Link, superintendent of the water department, urged residents in a statement yesterday to conserve water. This could make the difference, he said, as to whether the supply remains adequate enough to serve the people of the community without allocating specific quantities at certain times of the day.	Dansville, hit by drought, is so short of water that it may be cut off for times during the day unless everybody saves more, said Rolland Link, superintendent of the water department yesterday.

You may have noticed several common sources of wordiness. An abstract noun is used with an adjective when a simple adjective will do (of a far-reaching character); and an abstract noun is added to a concrete noun (slum conditions). Another source of wordiness is the change of a live verb into an abstract noun which then requires help from an adjective and a tame verb. Take the live-verb form:

He bowled badly.

That is a sentence with (pronoun) subject, verb and adverb. The adverb 'badly' is pale but it suffices. Compare the construction when the verb 'bowled' is made into the abstract noun 'bowling'. To say the same thing we then need a subject, noun, verb and adjective—and for some reason it is usually a woollier one.

His bowling was poor.

That is weaker—and longer. The deskman should restore purity to such sentences. Verb-adverb combinations are stronger and shorter than noun-verb-adjective combinations. Two verbs are better than verb plus abstract noun.

Here are some examples. Note that when a verb is rendered into a noun a group of abstract indirect words fastens on the corpse:

They will *conduct a survey of* an oasis.	They will survey an oasis.
They voted *for the expulsion of* . . .	They voted to expel . . .
A *parade will be held for the decoration of* the six men.	The six men will be decorated at a parade.
He favoured *the reorganisation of* . . .	He favoured reorganising . . .
Police *paid a visit to* the scene of the crime.	Police visited the scene of the crime.
Italy has *expressed a favourable attitude* toward *participating in studies on* the possible development of a NATO multilateral nuclear force, said a communique today. The United States has advocated the *creation of* such a force.	Italy favours . . . taking part/joining The United States has advocated this, or . . . advocated creating . . .
Objections have been raised by Macon County teachers.	Macon County teachers have objected.
He will *be responsible for the marshalling of* troops.	He will marshal troops.
They *made an estimation of the* value.	They estimated the value.

In the following example the deskman's antennae should have tingled at the approach of that abstract noun 'creation'. The original sentence is 44 words; the version on the right is only 26 words. Coast rescue is made the subject of the sentence because it identifies the topic at once in a more interesting way than beginning with an administrative body, the Medical Commission on Accident Prevention.

The creation of a national organisation to assist local authorities and voluntary societies and to bring a sense of urgency to the problem of rescue work around the coast of Britain is urged in the first report of the Medical Commission on Accident Prevention.	Coast rescue work urgently needs a national body to help voluntary societies and local authorities, says the first report of the Medical Commission on Accident Prevention.

Write with Nouns and Verbs

Some writers think that style means spraying adjectives and adverbs on sentences. These may give a superficial glitter. They often conceal rusty bodywork. Adjectives and adverbs should not be afterthoughts. They should be permitted only when they add precision and economy to a sentence. Every adjective should be examined to see: is it needed to define the subject or is it there for emphasis?

If something is amusing or sensational there is no need to tell the reader. The facts that amused or shocked should be described and he can apply his own adjectives. After all, as a newspaper style book years ago said, Genesis does not begin 'The amazingly dramatic story of how God made the world in the remarkably short time of six days . . .' Yet the worst kind of newspaper writing—said to be colourful—still cannot bear to let through a naked noun.

> In this *sunbaked* land lying between *strife-torn* Nigeria and *un-settled* Sudan, *dissident* Arab tribesmen of the *3,000-strong* CLF are badly rattling the *French-backed 6,000-strong* French Army.
> President Pompidou, who inherited the *thorny* problem of Chad from de Gaulle therefore faces an *acute* dilemma. France's prestige may suffer a *damaging* blow if the rebels win a *complete* victory . . .

It is extraordinary how much this kind of writing is improved simply by striking out the decoration, where the adjective is not defining but merely adorning—sunbaked, strife-torn, unsettled, dissident, thorny, acute, damaging, complete. The other phrases—3,000-strong, French-backed, and 6,000-strong—are economical ways of defining the noun, but in this sentence they merely add to the monotony of style. It would be better to say '. . . the 3,000-strong CLF are badly rattling the French-backed army of 6,000.'

Sports writers are still the gaudiest. 'This was the Portugal who crushed Brazil mercilessly from the World Cup, not the Portugal who so gracefully lost to England'.

That sentence is weakened, not strengthened, by the unnecessary *mercilessly*. And again: 'After a split second of *eerie* silence, the *thunderous* roars told him the *wonderful* news'. These adjectives do not define the nouns. They are there for effect. When there is a great deal of this the result is emasculating.

These are the sequins from one report. It was an exciting match when you could see it for the adjectives:

Magnificent; out of this world; their glowing skills and unflinching bravery; this man of magic; the thunder of exultant, rejoicing thousands; raked relentlessly through a shattered defence; an athletic immortal in his own golden age flicked in a shot that was a gem, a jewel of gold—no, a Crown Jewel; the golden dream; subdued and well-thrashed; so gallant and knightly; a disgrace to a noble competition; the red-and-white cauldron of Wembley bubbled joyously; the honest joy gleaming; faltered nervously; 53 tension-haunted minutes; typically outrageous; magnificently, gloriously, wonderfully, riotously.

It recalls Quiller-Couch's advice: 'Read over your compositions and when you meet a passage which you think is particularly fine, strike it out'.

It is not simply that some of the noun–adjective combinations here are cliché. The tedium of the automatic adjectives is too irritating; overemphasis destroys credibility. Deskmen should go to bed at night with Strunk's thought that the adjective has not been built that can pull a weak or inaccurate noun out of a tight place. Superlatives should be put through a second sieve for accuracy. The biggest, tallest, fastest, richest so often turns out to be the second biggest, second tallest, second fastest and second richest.[5]

These are some adjectives which are absolute, and modifications should be challenged:

absolute, certain, complete, devoid, empty, entire, essential, external, everlasting, excellent, fatal, final, full, fundamental, harmless, ideal, immaculate, immortal, impossible, incessant, indestructible, infinite, invaluable, invulnerable, main, omnipotent, perfect, principal, pure, simultaneous, ultimate, unanimous, unendurable, unique, unspeakable, untouchable, whole, worthless.

Strike out Meaningless Modifiers

No word should be encumbered with a parasite, consuming space and debasing the language. It is absurd when the word is an absolute. An incident is either unique or it is not. It cannot be 'rather' unique. It is like

---

[5] If it is not in the *Guinness Book of Records* do not award a superlative you cannot defend to the satisfaction of all offended parties.

being 'rather pregnant'. A seller monopolises a market or he does not. It is meaningless to report him as having 'absolutely' (or 'partly') 'monopolised the market'. If the copy says the pitch had reached 'a high degree of perfection', the deskman should pass only the fact that the pitch is near-perfect (as in truth it probably isn't perfect). If something is inevitable, it cannot be more or most inevitable. It cannot be nearly inevitable.

The 'lonely hermit' could have been nothing else. To report 'the final outcome' suggests, ridiculously that there could have been a half-way outcome. It is no satisfaction to those turned away to read that the theatre was 'completely' full.

Many non-absolutes are weakened by qualifiers. Danger is danger, and a good strong word, but often in newspapers you see reports of 'serious' and 'real' danger. Real may be justified if an imaginary danger is contrasted; but whoever heard of an unserious danger? Sir Ernest Gowers in his admirable book for civil servants[6] nailed another abuse in the qualifications 'due' and 'undue'. 'The tenants were asked not to be unduly alarmed'. As Gowers says, it differs little from 'there is no cause for alarm for which there is no cause' and that hardly seems worth saying.

Here are some newspaper examples (my italics); comments or re-writes are on the right. Later on in this chapter there is a longer list of redundancies.

At an *annual* value of £1 million *a year*.	Either 'a year' or 'annual' is superfluous.
Some of the remarks made *included* . . .	The remarks included . . .
He agreed to *augment* the *existing* watchman force from five to seven men.	The watchmen must already exist, or they could not be augmented.
Michael Salter, aged 4, was scalded on both legs by *hot* water in his home today.	Hardly with cold.
Johnson discarded *two other possible alternatives* as being impracticable.	If they weren't possible, they would not be alternatives.

---

[6] *Plain Words*, by Sir Ernest Gowers (London: HM Stationery Office, 1948).

| He said a driving test was an *essential condition*. | If it's a condition it must be essential: He said a driving test was essential. |
| A *growing* gulf seems to be *developing*. | A gulf seems to be developing. |

A further source of wordiness is in descriptions of quantities or measure. Simplicity and directness call for *many, some, few, most, heavy, light, short, long*. What the deskman often sees on copy is *in the majority of instances, in a number of cases, a large proportion of*. He should never hesitate to change these prolix forms. 'A large percentage of failures' should be changed to 'many failures'. He should also always be ready to question modifying and deprecating phrases. Sir Ernest Gowers detected that writers feel there is something indecent about the unadorned adjectives 'few', 'short', and so on. Adverbial dressing gowns are thrown around these naked adjectives—*unduly, relatively, comparatively*. Yet often there is nothing to compare, and the qualification is meaningless as well as space-consuming. Check: is there a real comparison in the story? If there is not, off with the dressing gown!

The deskman should also suspect *in more or less degree, somewhat, to a certain extent, to a degree, small in size, quite,* and that news accretion *mark*: 'The death roll has topped the 300 mark'. Why 'mark'? It should be reported: 'More than 300 have died'.

Avoid Needless Repetition

The most noticeable needless repetition, rife especially throughout the US press and the Associated Press wire service, is repetition of source. Once the report has identified the source of the information there is no need to keep parading it. Only if identity is in doubt need it be repeated.

> The United States is ready to sell the Soviet Union 200 bushels of wheat for $380 million in cash, *U.S. Secretary Of Agriculture*, Orville Freeman, indicated yesterday. *Freeman* cautioned that no decision had been made. *The agriculture secretary* came to Harrisburg following a meeting with the President on the wheat sale question. Though *Freeman* said no deal had been closed. . . .

The constant drip of the source is like Chinese water torture. Nowhere does it seem to have occurred to the copyreader that there is such
a thing as a pronoun. And again:

Fire early today wrecked the marina in Brooman, causing an estimated £10,000 of damage, *police said*. *The fire* destroyed the main building and an *undetermined number* of boats, *said police*.

'Police said.' Do we doubt them?

It destroyed the main building and *some* boats.

Some deskmen and reporters exhibit in their copy the kind of phobia
that makes us go downstairs ten times to check that the light is off. They
have a nagging doubt that the reader has not quite got the point—so
they keep going on about it. Once is enough for most pieces of information. When the information is merely incidental its repetition is doubly
irritating.

Here is a report, from an English provincial daily, of a speech at a
factory opening:

A Government grant to promote publicity for the North-East will be announced in Parliament today.

This was revealed by Mr George Chetwynd, Director of the North-East Development Council, after he had opened a new £300,000 particle board plant at the Willington Quay factory of the Tyne Board Company Limited yesterday.

'I cannot disclose the amount of the grant until it has been presented to Parliament', said Mr Chetwynd. 'But it will be a highly satisfactory figure. It will enable us to do a much bigger and better job in the area than we have been able so far.'

The factory which Mr Chetwynd was opening . . .

While Mr Chetwynd declared the plant open in the presence of . . .

Mr Chetwynd, before pushing the button to start the new plant, said he believed 1964 would be a turning point in the future of Tyneside . . .

The new plant opened by Mr Chetwynd will produce . . .

Does anybody want to argue about whether Mr Chetwynd opened that plant?

Why, in the next story, do we have the repetition of 'people'? If it were a story about asthma striking elephants and people, it would be worth making the point. Otherwise it can be left understood after the first reference that the report is about people. Better still, the noun 'people' should be translated into individuals—elderly men, or young children, or women and children. The meaning of the version on the right is clear and it saves 17 words.

The Cuban radio reported today that three more *people* have died from a peculiar type of asthma attack that struck down more than 200 *people* in Havana. Five *people* died of asthma on Wednesday because of a freak atmospheric condition, according to the radio which was monitored in Miami.	Three more people died from a peculiar asthma that has struck down more than 200 in Havana, says Cuban Radio. Five died of asthma on Wednesday night because of freak atmospheric conditions.

Avoid Monologophobia

The world is indebted to Theodore Bernstein of the *New York Times* for this term which has the virtue that it is ugly enough to spring out of the page and hit you. A monologophobe, says Mr Bernstein[7], is a guy who would rather walk naked in front of Saks Fifth Avenue than be caught using the same word more than once in three lines of type. Some of the writers stricken with monologophobia are the ones who had an aversion (in the preceding section) to the humble pronoun; their remedy is to invent another noun. Here are two examples:

Palestine's Arabs swore before the United Nations special Palestine committee today to drench the soil of that tiny country 'with the last drop of our blood' in opposing any big power scheme to partition the Holy Land.

---

[7] *Watch Your Language* (New York: Channel Press, 1958), p. 132.

> The Minister of Transport, Mrs
> Barbara Castle, today opened a new
> motorway extension to Preston. The
> red-headed non-driver said two
> more extensions were planned and
> by 1970 it would be possible to drive
> the 150 miles without entering a
> single town. The Minister, who sits
> for Blackburn, travelled . . .

One country is given three different names: Palestine, that tiny country, and the Holy Land. The insertion of the synonym 'red-headed non-driver' for Mrs Castle leaves the reader wondering if he is still reading about the same person. Fowler, who called this 'elegant variation,' thought minor novelists and reporters were the real victims 'first terrorized by a misunderstood taboo, next fascinated by a newly discovered ingenuity, and finally addicted to an incurable vice'[8]. The fatal influence is certainly the advice given to young writers never to use the same word twice in a sentence. A monologophobe would edit the Bible so that you would read, 'Let there be light and there was solar illumination'.

The leather sphere seems to have disappeared from the sports pages, but monologophobia strikes in many places. In court reports there is a bewildering alternation of the names of people with their status as 'defendant' or 'plaintiff'. It is better to stick to names throughout:

> The lorry driver said he was going
> towards Finchley when he saw the
> deceased suddenly walk into the
> road.

The most frequent symptom of monologophobia in British newspapers is the aversion to the good verb 'to say'. According to what you read, people don't *say* things any more, they:

> point out that, express the opinion, express the view, indicate, observe, state, explain, report, continue, add, declare . . .

People don't *tell* other people things. They inform, notify and communicate. The worst variation is the casual smear when the deskman or writer substitutes 'admit' for 'say'. To 'admit' something in public has different overtones from simply saying it: it implies confession for some

[8] *A Dictionary of Modern English Usage*, by H W Fowler (Oxford University Press, 2nd edition, 1965), p. 148.

wrong. That verb should rarely be used outside court reports. If someone does not deny a point put to him it is better to say 'he agreed that ...'

The verb 'to claim' is another bad synonym: it implies that we have
our doubts. All such variants should be used only when they express
meaning more accurately. Let someone 'affirm' a fact only when it has
been in doubt. Never let anybody 'declare' what is clearly an informal
remark. Emphatically it does not mutilate the language to use 'he said'
twice in a report. What does mutilate the language is to say 'he explained'
when the man is clearly not explaining anything at all.

Monologophobia is aggravated by the other writing sin of converting
a verb into an abstract noun, or transforming a specific noun into an
abstract noun. People don't hope; they 'express hope'. They don't
believe; they 'indicate belief'. And here is an example from an evening
newspaper monologophobe:

> With more staff available for after-
> care at home, the Swindon Mater-
> nity Hospital, dealing with an in-
> creasing number of *admissions*, will
> be able to send some mothers home
> earlier.

Are the 'admissions' the same people as the 'mothers'? Why, yes; no
fathers have been patients at Swindon Maternity Hospital. So the
report should have conceded at once that it is about mothers—a specific
and human noun clearly more interesting than the abstract 'admissions':
'Some mothers will go home earlier from busy Swindon Maternity
Home'.

That is what the report is about. But such reasoning takes time and
patience, and some monologophobes are more readily cunning in creating bewilderment for the reader.

Monologophobia is related also to over-attribution (*see* p. 45). Even
the pronoun cannot redeem this fault. Part of the trouble is often inept
handling of reported speech. But where there is only once source it is
clear who is speaking and the deskman should strike out from copy those
'he continued', 'he added' and 'he explained' variations.

> There is no question of any of
> GEC's 2,000 workers being de-
> moted because they fail an aptitude
> test, said Mr. E. M. Cowley, the
> firm's divisional manager last night.
> Aptitude tests, *he explained*, were

part of the firm's normal routine. They were to see if people were fitted for promotion, not to see if anyone should move down, *he continued.*

'If there are openings we believe in considering the available resources first', *said Mr. Cowley.*

The words in italics could all be deleted without difficulty here. After 'move down' in the second paragraph, there would be a colon followed by the quotation.

Watch the Prepositions

There are three troubles: the circumlocutory preposition; the prepositional verb; and pedantry.

The circumlocutory preposition is a fluffy substitute for the single preposition which gives the meaning as clearly. The worst offenders are in the field of, in connection with, in order to, in respect of, with regard to, in relation to, with reference to, in the case of, so far as . . . is concerned. All sorts of things are found flourishing in the field of: in the field of public relations, in the field of breakfast cereals, in the field of book publishing, in the field of nuts and bolts . . .

'Field' has a very proper association with battle, chivalry and war (hence 'Never in the field of human conflict . . .'), but the word is usually superfluous when used generally. These are newspaper examples, with my amendments and comments on the right:

This and other developments in medical science are at the base of a dialogue now proceeding in the Roman Catholic Church *concerning* its attitude to medical aids *in the field of birth control.*

This and other developments in medicine are at the base of a dialogue in the Roman Catholic Church *on* its attitude to medical aids *in birth control.*

More progress has been made *in the case of* Southern Rhodesia.

More progress has been made *with* Rhodesia.

Arnold Wesker's Chips with Everything is a bitter attack on the class system that leaves much to be desired *as far as satisfactory drama is concerned.*

i.e. dramatically.

The rates vary *in relation to* the value of the building.

The rates vary *with* the value of the building.

In connection with a recruiting exhibition at Scarborough, the famous team of Royal Corps of Signals motor cyclists gave a display.	As part of a recruiting exhibition at Scarborough . . .

Prepositional verbs grow like toadstools. Once there was credit in facing a problem. Now problems have to be faced *up to*. The prepositions add nothing to significance. To say one met somebody is plain enough; to say one met *up with* them adds nothing and takes two further words. So it is with win (out); consult (with); stop (off); check (up on); divide (up); test (out).

The prepositions are American parasites. Mostly they can be deleted, or replaced by a simple alternative verb. Call is better than stop off at; fit, reach or match will serve better than measure up to. There is strength in a few prepositional verbs such as get on with; go back on; take up with. But most of the modern currency is American dumping which weakens English. It is a poor day when it is no longer considered enough to say honesty pays. Inflation requires honesty to pay *off*; and we are the worse for it.

The third trouble with the preposition is the influence of the pedants. They insist that prepositions must never end a sentence. The preposition, it is said, should always be placed before the word it governs. This is an attempt to impose on English some of the rigour of Latin and it will not do. Shakespeare wrote of 'the heartache and the thousand natural shocks that flesh is heir to'. That is good English. Fowler dealt trenchantly with the pedantry of the preposition but it flourishes in official, legal and police court language. Policemen are apt to say 'The water into which he dived', and lawyers 'The contract into which he entered'.

Pedants would frown on 'The pilot said it depended on what they were guided by'. Trying to tuck that preposition 'by' back where it is supposed to belong produces a sentence everyone ought to frown on: 'The pilot said it depended on by what they were guided'. As Fowler observed, 'too often the lust of sophistication, once blooded, becomes uncontrollable', and you end up with 'The pilot said that depended on the answer to the question as to by what they were guided'.

The best advice is to forget the Latin and accept what sounds most comfortable to the educated ear. It sounds better to say the prepositional pedants are people not worth listening to; better than to say these pedants are people to whom it is not worth listening.

Care for Meanings

'When *I* use a word', Humpty-Dumpty told Alice, 'it means just what I choose it to mean, neither more nor less'. The Humpties of the written word present two problems to the deskman. Writers give new meanings to old words; and new expressions are being created all the time.

Disinterested is often used in an ambiguous way. Its correct meaning is not bored or uninterested, but impartial or unselfish. But when we read 'The President said he would be disinterested in the conflict', what are we to understand? It should mean the President will stay interested but neutral. To most of us it will. But to some—and perhaps to the writer—it means the President is bored with the conflict and will take no further interest. Here the deskman should be a stickler for accuracy. He should not let a good word down. But what shall be his attitude to blurb, kickback, crack down, beat it, to bus, killjoy, cheap skate, gate-crash? It would be a mistake to maintain the pedantry required to protect the old words. The English language has a genius for such vivid new idiom, particularly in American hands. This is an act of creation, the combination of familiar verbs, prepositions, pronouns and conjunctions into rich new images.

It is very different from the act of distortion which destroys disinterested, alibi, immigrant, enervated, chronic and so on. The essential difference is that there is often universal understanding of new idiom and the best of it fills a real need. It comes into being precisely to describe an idea more economically and vividly than the existing vocabulary allows: 'He put it across'; 'He is a killjoy'; 'They do it for kicks'.

It is easy enough for the deskman to admit old words on condition that they are travelling in their own name: there are dictionaries to detect imposters. It is harder to verify the passports of new expressions. Webster's dictionary in its 1961 Third Edition argued that almost anything goes if somebody uses it. But that is too loose. 'Simple illiteracy', as Dwight Macdonald said, 'is no basis for linguistic evolution'.

There are two tests: Does the expression represent a new idea? Does it do it more briefly or precisely than the old expressions? Much new idiom will for these reasons vanish after a temporary popularity; and the deskman should certainly help it on its way. Not all contemporary catchwords are clear signals: some modern ones seem, indeed, only to add to the confusion. Is a 'hang up' a stimulant or a hangover, does 'uptight' convey proximity or a state of mind, is 'too much, man' a term of approval or disapproval and does 'fabulous' mean anything more than 'I like it'? 'A depressed socioeconomic area' does not say anything which slum said more briefly before; transportation is longer than transport; so is for free instead of free; to author is not better than to write; senior citizen is longer and more pretentious than old man or pensioner; finalisation is a rough usurper for finish or completion; telly is longer than TV. The suffix 'wise' as in bookwise and verbwise should also, wisdomwise, have a short life; but in all these judgments humility is in order. Our language is not the language of Chaucer, and the good words mob, bamboozle, sham, bully, banter, and uppish, were all originally denounced as vulgar slang by the great Jonathan Swift.

Here are some of the words commonly misused in newspapers. This is a taste of the range of abuse. There are other sources[9] and the slightest whiff of doubt should send the deskman to the dictionary.

Affect: Confused, as verb, with effect. To effect is to bring about, to affect is to change. To say 'it effected a change in his attitude' is correct; so is 'it affected his attitude.' To combine the two—'It affected a change in his attitude'—is wrong.

Alibi: Means 'otherwise' or elsewhere, but is confused with excuse, which is a wider term. Alibi means being somewhere else when the deed was done.

Alternatives: Wrongly used for choices. If there are two choices, they are properly called alternatives. If there are more than two they are choices.

Anticipate: Confused with expect. To expect something is to think it may happen; to anticipate is to prepare for it, to act in advance. To say a fiancée expects marriage is correct; to say she is anticipating it is defamatory.

Anxious: Best preserved as meaning troubled, uneasy. It is a corruption to use it as a synonym for eager or desirous.

Breach: To break through or break a promise or rule. But to breech, with an e, means to put a boy into trousers.

Causal: Perhaps the hardest word to get into a newspaper—everybody thinks it ought to be 'casual': it means relating to a cause, and is often used in philosophical or medical contexts.

[9] In particular the *Concise Usage and Abusage*, by Eric Partridge (London: Hamish Hamilton, 1954), and *Doing it in Style*, by Leslie Sellers (Oxford: Pergamon Press, 1968), p. 166.

Celebrant: Confused with celebrator. A celebrant presides over a religious rite.

Chronic: Confused with acute or severe. It means long-lasting (from the Greek *chronos*—time), medically usually the opposite: an acute illness comes to a crisis, a chronic one lingers.

Cohort: Confused with henchman. A cohort is a company of warriors, or people banded together. You cannot sensibly say 'Smith came with his cohort Brown'.

Comprise: Confused with composes. Comprise means to contain or include. The whole comprises the parts. The United States comprises 50 states; 50 states do not comprise the United States. Contains, includes or consists of are preferable.

Cozening: Confused with cosseting. To be cosseted is to be petted or pampered. To be cozened, on the other hand, is to be cheated or defrauded.

Credible: Confused with credulous. A credible man is one you can believe; a credulous man, however, is too ready to believe others.

Crescendo: Confused with climax. It indicates a passage of music to be played with increasing volume. Figuratively, it means to rise to a climax. Thus the cliché 'rise to a crescendo' is nonsense.

Decimate: Confused with destroy. By derivation decimation means killing one in ten. Today it is often used figuratively to mean very heavy casualties, but to say 'completely decimated' or 'decimated as much as half the town' simply will not do.

Dependent/Dependant: A dependant is a person who is dependent on another for support.

Deprecate: Confused with depreciate. An MP was reported as depreciating sterling as a world currency. That means he had it devalued, which is the job of the Governor of the Bank of England. What the MP did was deprecate sterling as a world currency, i.e. plead against the policy.

Dilemma: Confused with problem. If you have a problem you do not know what to do. There may be many solutions. If you have a dilemma you have a choice of two courses of action, both unfavourable.

Discomfit: Confused with discomfort. To discomfort is to make uneasy; to discomfit is to defeat or rout. Discomfort is either verb or noun; the noun of discomfit is discomfiture.

Discrete: Confused with discreet. The discrete object is separate, distinct (and it is better to say so). The discreet man is tactful.

Disinterested: Confused with uninterested, but instead means impartial, i.e. not having a sectional or vested interest.

Enervate: Confused with energise. It means the opposite. To enervate is to weaken, to energise is to invigorate. The *New York Times* did Mr Arnold Weinstock an injustice: 'Two years later after a power struggle at the top, Mr Weinstock emerged as managing director at the age of 38. He then enervated his company with his now-familiar technique.'

Entomb: Confused with entrap. The entrapped miners may be alive; entombed miners are dead, i.e. in a tomb.

Exotic: Means 'of foreign origin' and only by weak analogy 'glamorous' or 'colourful': a Sicilian peasant is as exotic as Gina Lollobrigida.

Explicit: Confused with implicit. It means the opposite. An explicit understanding has been expressed. An implicit understanding has been left implied, not expressly stated.

Flaunt: Confused with flout. 'We must not allow the American constitution to be flaunted in this way . . .' means we must not allow it to be paraded, displayed or shown off. That is the meaning of to flaunt. What the speaker intended to say was that the constitution should not be flouted, i.e. mocked or insulted.

Forego: Confused with forgo. Forego means to go before in time or place—think of the final e in before. To forgo is to give up, or relinquish.

Fulsome: Confused with full. Fulsome means overfull, extravagant, to the point of insincerity. To say 'He gave her fulsome praise' is to make a comment on its merits.

Further: Confused with farther. Keep farther for distances—thus far and no farther—and further for additions (furthermore).

Immigrant: In Britain it has become a euphemism for a coloured man. It should be rescued for what it is—anyone from abroad who has come to settle. It is not the same, either, as alien. An immigrant is a settler, an alien may be a visitor.

Inflammable: Confused with inflammatory. Words may be inflammatory—they may cause - metaphorical fire—but they are not inflammable. The paper on which they are written, however, may be combustible, or liable to burn, and therefore inflammable (flammable would be better, but does not have wide currency).

Invaluable: Confused with valueless, which is the opposite. The invaluable stone cannot be priced because it has so much value it is priceless. The valueless stone is worthless.

Involved: Overworked and misused. Involved is best preserved to mean tangled, complicated. It should not replace verbs like include, entail, implicate, affect, imply, engage. We should say 'the scheme *entails* knocking down ten houses'; 'four hundred men are *engaged* in the strike'—or 'four hundred are *on strike* or *affected*'; and 'so-and-so is *implicated* in the crime,' and so on.

Judicious: Confused with judicial. Judicial means connected with a court of law, judicious means wise. Not all judicial decisions are judicious.

Lay: Confused with lie. Hens lay eggs, men lay traps and lay down burdens. The dog lies down on the ground: let sleeping dogs lie. Men lie down themselves, lie in prison for years and lie in state. Much of the confusion is because the past tense of lie is lay. The correct forms are lie-lay-lain; lay-laid-laid.

Less: Confused with fewer. Less is right for quantities—less coffee, less sugar. It means a less amount of. Fewer is right for comparing numbers—fewer people, fewer houses, less dough means fewer loaves. Nobody would think of saying fewer coffee, fewer sugar, but every day somebody writes less houses.

Licence: The noun is confused with the verb license.

Literally: Confused with metaphorically. This provides umpteen nonsense statements. We were literally flooded with books. He literally went up in smoke. He literally exploded in anger. Literally means exactness to the letter. To say he literally went up in smoke means he was burned, exploded, etc.

Livid: Confused with angry: livid means lead-coloured, but some angry people are very pale.

Loan: Confused with lend. Loan is the noun, lend the verb. The moneylender lends, and so makes you a loan.

Luxuriant: Confused with luxurious. The film star can have a luxurious car which is full of luxury, but not a luxuriant car. That means a car which is producing abundantly, growing profusely. Luxuriant refers to something that grows.

Mitigate: Confused with militate. It is said, incorrectly, that an act will mitigate against a settlement. But mitigate means to appease, to soften. It is militate which is intended—to make war or tell against. Think of military.

None: Means not one or no one and takes a singular verb (just as other distributive expressions like each, each one, everybody, everyone, many a man, nobody).

Oblivious: Confused with ignorant of. Oblivious is from the Latin *oblivium*, meaning forgetfulness. If you are ignorant of something, nobody told you. If you are oblivious, somebody told you but you let it slip into oblivion.

Practice: In English usage, practice is the noun, to practise, practising, practised the verb.

Principle: Confused with principal. The principal is first in rank or importance; principle is a fundamental source or moral conviction. The Principal has principles.

Protagonist: Confused with antagonist and with champion. Literally it means the leading character in a drama; it does not mean advocate or champion. Somebody can be a protagonist without advocating anything. An antagonist is an active opponent.

Quota: It means an allotted number, akin to rationing. To say New York had its full quota of rain means somebody was assigning various amounts of rain to New York.

Recrudescence: Confused with resurgence. 'There was a resurgence of loyalty' is right. To say 'there was a recrudescence of loyalty' is to misuse a good metaphor. Recrudescence means the breaking out of a sore or disease and it should be used, figuratively, for disagreeable events.

Regalia: Regal means of or by kings, and regalia means the insignia of royalty. Royal regalia is therefore tautologous and 'the regalia of a bishop' is contradictory. Freemasons, however, have adopted the term for their insignia.

Replica: Confused with reproduction. A replica is a duplicate or exact copy made by the original artist; anyone can attempt a reproduction.

Stationary: Confused with stationery. Stationary, adjective, is static; stationery, noun, is writing materials.

Synthetic: Is not a synonym for false as in 'a synthetic excuse'. It means 'placed together', from the Greek *syn*, together, and *tithemi*, place. Think of synthetic rubber, made by placing its constituents together, rather than by extraction from a plant.

Titivate: Confused with titillate. To titivate is to adorn or smarten. The seducer may do that to himself, but he will seek to titillate the victim—to excite pleasantly.

Transpired: Wrongly used to mean something merely happened. It comes from the Latin *spirare*, breathe. To transpire is to emit through the lungs or skin and, figuratively, is best used for when some fact, especially a secret, oozes out.

Urbane: Confused with urban. Urban means of the city; urbane means courteous, suave. Not all people in urban areas are urbane.

Viable: Misused as a substitute for feasible or practicable. Viable means capable of independent life—a viable foetus, or seed, or, figuratively, scheme.

Vice: It would be a pity if it became a synonym for sex. There are many vices. It should be used as the opposite of virtue.

Virtually: Incorrectly used to mean nearly all, e.g. virtually all the chocolates were eaten. Virtually usefully means in essence or effect 'as contrasted to formality'. 'He's virtually the manager'. He does not have the title but he manages the business.

While: It means, strictly, during the time that; it is also tolerable as although, but. (While seeing your point, I cannot give you permission.) But it is nonsense to use while as a synonym for *and* or *whereas*. 'Mr Jones is the president while Mr Smith is the secretary', means Jones is president during the time that Smith is secretary. It means they must resign together. Sir Alan Herbert exposes the absurdity: 'The curate read the first lesson while the rector read the second'.

Avoid Cliches

The first million writers (or cave-painters) who told us about their 'thorny problems' used metaphor vividly. The prickliness of their position was plain to see. Some time after that the prickliness became less apparent; excessive use of the metaphor blunted it. The adjective had become a passenger. The cliché had been born.

To enjoin writers never to use a cliché is to anticipate a definition and to seek the impossible. Perhaps we can define a cliché as any phrase 'so hackneyed as to be knock-kneed and spavined'[10]. There are a lot of them about. There are no doubt some in this book. It is impossible to ban them, because they serve a natural inclination. At best they are a form of literary shorthand, with the attraction of economy. Is it better to say 'he was bustling and industrious' than 'he was busy as a bee'? What deskmen can do with clichés in copy is to ration them, and tolerate only the best. They are worst where they seek to enliven dull patches; but they do nothing of the sort. The imagery is dead. The worst are wasteful, too. 'In deadly earnest' says no more than 'in earnest', 'to all intents and purposes' says no more than 'virtually'. In my list (pp. 80–83) are the commonest newspaper clichés which should all be treated with hostility.

Story Sources of Wordiness

Suggestions for conciser and more human news stories have been set out in terms of words and sentences. Certain kinds of news stories throw up their own wordiness and the way these stories should be edited will be examined now.

Reported speech   Editing speeches and documents requires an adroit combination of direct and indirect reporting. Direct speech ('Accordingly I shall not seek and I will not accept the nomination of my party for another term as your President') has the advantage of accuracy and liveliness. It has the disadvantage of taking a lot of space. Reported speech (Mr Johnson said he will not run again) is the great economiser.

The reporting of official documents and other statements is best done in third-person summary: to rely on direct quotation is to miss the opportunity to render officialese into economic English which touches people's lives. Speeches, too, require third-person reporting, but not as much. The more important the speech, the more space should be given to direct quotation. If only one section of a speech is newsworthy, it is preferable to give that whole section in quotes in original sequence and indicate in third person that other subjects were discussed. It is very frustrating for the reader to have only the third-person summary of a key

[10] See *A Dictionary of Cliches*, by Eric Partridge (London: Routledge, 1940).

passage. This is perhaps the worst defect of modern reporting of speeches, a reflection perhaps of shortage of space, lack of seriousness and the failure of the young journalist to master the basic tool of short-hand.

Direct quotes, then, should be preferred—but when it is necessary to use third person for summarising, it is necessary to use it ruthlessly and not render into third person the speaker's verbosity, circumlocutions, cough and all.

Third-person reporting is a skill. It demands both fidelity to the material and a determination to use indirect speech as a knife to cut through to the real content. Fidelity demands that interpretation should be scrupulously accurate. If a speaker makes a statement which is a rebuke, that will be self-evident from its context. If it is not self-evident, then there must be some doubt; but it is dangerous for deskmen to resolve the doubt by saying so-and-so rebuked or attacked or criticised. The speaker's words should speak for themselves.

The third-person summary should be true to the meaning and spirit of the material. If the news point is taken from a few minutes or passages at the end, that should be indicated: 'Mr X's comments on incomes came in the last few minutes of a speech mainly defending government policy . . .'

There is no doubt that on occasion clumsy reported speech can do violence to a speaker's tone and ideas. Sometimes the articulate are rendered incoherent and a grand survey is turned into a mish-mash of unrelated thoughts. Here is a piece of reported speech which is extreme but has the virtue of encompassing most of the defects found singly elsewhere:

> When the Language Commission was appointed for the purpose of considering the various steps to be taken under Article 344, Mr Subramaniam continued, the Government of Madras had to consider the whole question and give a lead and submit a memorandum to the Commission. He pointed out that the one point which was considered by them more than once was whether they should seek a Constitutional amendment or they should take the stand that if only the safeguards in Part 17 were properly formulated and worked in the proper spirit it would be possible to meet the various problems arising out of the language problem. They came to the conclusion that it would be possible for them to have all the safeguards worked out under the provisions of the Constitution. As a matter of fact, this matter was again considered when the Language Commission had submitted its report because the Commission had almost ignored most of the major recommendations

made by the State Government in their memorandum.

They again came to the conclusion that it might not be necessary to press for a Constitutional amendment if only the other authorities which might be considering the question, namely the Parliamentary Committee, which had to be constituted to consider the recommendations of the Commission, also later the President, who had to pass an order based on the recommendations of the Language Commission, and the Parliamentary Committee, took note of what they would be submitting further. It was only on that basis that the second memorandum was prepared and submitted to the Parliamentary Committee, they said. Mr Subramaniam said fortunately for them, the Parliamentary Committee had taken note of the various points they had made in their Second Memorandum and almost accepted all the recommendations they had made.

There is no place in a newspaper for the speaker's wordiness—'for the purpose'; 'as a matter of fact'; 'came to the conclusion'; 'recommendations they had made'; 'arising out of'. These are understandable, if unfortunate, in speech; as written words they are glaringly superfluous. Everything in that report is preserved in this third-person version of the speech—which saves about 200 words:

Mr Subramaniam said that when the Language Commission was appointed to consider the steps necessary under Article 344, the Madras Government had to give its views. Madras debated whether it should seek a Constitutional amendment or whether the problems could be met by observing the safeguards of Part 17 in a proper spirit. They decided there were enough safeguards in the existing Constitution.

The Language Commission 'almost ignored' most of the major recommendations of the State Government, said Mr Subramaniam, but Madras again decided it might not be necessary to press for a Constitutional amendment if only their recommendations would be heeded by the Parliamentary Committee and by the President who had to act on the report of both the Language Commission and the Parliamentary Committee.

Fortunately the Parliamentary Committee had accepted most of the State Government's recommendations.

It is possible, of course to boil this down even further:

Mr Subramaniam recalled that Madras had decided to put its trust in Part 17. They had stuck to this view even when the Language Commission 'almost ignored' them because they knew they would get a hearing from the Parliamentary Committee on the Language Commission's report. They did and the Parliamentary Committee had accepted almost all the points Madras made.

Here is an example from a South African newspaper. No doubt Dr Donges did say what was reported, but it would have done no violence to his meaning for the deskman to put into print the version on the right:

Dr Donges said he was pleased to say it could not be denied that South Africa had made important progress in the economic sphere.	Dr Donges said South Africa had made important economic progress.

Where a speaker or report changes subject the reporter often strives for continuity by his own clumsy transition phrases: 'Turning to the question of . . .', 'Dealing with the subject of . . .' or 'Referring to the . . .'. It is far better to deal briskly with changes of subject, especially lower in a report, with simple phrases 'On sterling, Mr. Heath said . . .'. And again: 'Of President de Gaulle, Dean Rusk said . . .'. Alternatively, in tighter editing the deskman can mark separate paragraphs on the copy in this style:

These were the report's other comments:

VIETNAM: 'We must continue to support the United States'.

OVERSEAS AID: The time had not arrived for reductions.

Similarly where a deskman is dealing with a complicated Bill or White Paper, he should seek to enumerate key points, listing items 1, 2, 3 and so on in separate paragraphs.

A speaker should always be identified early in the story by name and status (Mr J. Bloggs of the Meat Grinders' Guild) and later by location (speaking at a mass rally at the Albert Hall, London). Where there is more than one speaker, each new speaker should have a new paragraph —beginning with his name. There is no other way. If the name comes anywhere other than in the first line the reader will assume that the previous speaker is still on his feet.

Direct quotation Good quotes are the lifeblood of the news columns. In ordinary news stories when people are interviewed they do not normally come out with a series of neat, colourful sentences which sum up the whole action. A few of their quotes have to be woven into a story in reported speech. But the good quotes must be treasured; they have the pungency of personal experience. The reporter back from the fire weakened his story by the third-person summary, 'The merchant foresaw the prospect of ruin', which was inferior to (and longer than) what the man actually said: 'This could ruin me'.

The set speech should provide a higher proportion of salvageable quotations than the casual interview, and higher still than the official report. Quotations from speeches should be given to:

● Support statements given in the intro in reported speech

● Capture the subtleties of important or controversial statements, or ones that show a speaker's richness of language

● Report lively exchanges between speaker and heckler, judge and lawyer, and so on

● Change the pace in a long section of third-person reporting.

Here is the first category in practice:

> Mr Sidney Silverman, the veteran left-winger, who has been in trouble with his party chiefs more than once, yesterday condemned as undemocratic Mr Wilson's discipline speech to back-benchers.
>
> Mr Silverman, in a letter to the chief whip, said Mr Wilson's doctrine on the submission of Labour back-benchers was 'the most dangerous attack on social democracy in this country in my time'.

The quote there is vital to support the intro: indeed it ought to have been in the intro. But what is rarely necessary is to give the reader in quotes in the body of the story the identical statement he has already been offered in third-person reporting; or vice-versa:

> Canon L. John Collins, Precentor at St. Paul's Cathedral, said in his sermon yesterday: 'I cannot refrain from commenting upon the extraordinary service of thanksgiving which took place in St. Vedast's in the City, on Thursday, attended

by the Board of Courtaulds and a
hundred or so of their employees'.

He asked what connection the
service could have with the Christian gospel which condemned outright the system which made possible the fight between ICI and
Courtaulds.

'One must ask what connection
the service can have had with the
Christian gospel which condemns
outright the whole system which
makes possible such a fight'.

Once is enough, twice is a feast, three times is a felony.

Micky Mantle, the New York Yan-
kees' 100,000-dollar-a-year out-
fielder with the dime store legs, said
yesterday—the eve of the World
Series opener—that he may be
forced into a post-session operation
on his left leg.

'If it doesn't get any better', said
Mantle before taking a workout at
Yankee Stadium, *it'll have to be
operated on*. It's been getting stronger day by day, but as it stands now,
we think *it's going to be operated on*'.

Here is an example which uses both direct quotation and reported
speech wastefully:

Plans call *for the construction of* a
one-storey ambulance headquarters
building, for which materials and
labour will be *donated* by con-
tractors, Gates Police Chief William
Stauber said.

'Several sites, I'm happy to say,
have been offered free of charge for
the headquarters structure and we
are now in the process of determining which would be the best location.'

Why should Police Chief William Stauber be allowed to gulp mouthfuls
of newsprint with 'in the process of determining which would be the
best location' etc., when they're simply thinking of where to build the
thing?

There are two final cautions on quotes. Deskmen should not alter
quotes and reporters should not invent them. By invention I do not

mean the completely fictitious quotation dreamed up by Lunch Time O'Booze, which is rare, but the temptation to attribute to direct quotation what is only an acknowledgment of a question. If the words are in quotes they must be the words the speaker has said himself. That is the point of the marks. If he has merely said 'Yes' to a long colourful question, then the report should only say 'He agreed that . . .'. It is permissible for reporter or deskman to change the order of sentences to make a statement more coherent, but the sense and individual wording must not be altered.

The commonest fault is to have people saying things more emphatically than they did. The deskman's temptation is to edit the quotations produced by the reporter, which gives a second risk of distortion. Deletion within quotes is justified only if the omission of the words is indicated by dots. It has to be judged carefully. Qualifications should not be dropped. Alteration of words within quotes is inexcusable. If the quotes do not add anything the answer is not to improve the quotation but to delete it altogether and revert to reported speech or to pick up only the attractive phrase or word in quotes in a combination of reported speech and quotes.

> Prince Philip warned that the selfish approach to conservation would lead to our generation being 'loathed and despised by all who come after us till the end of time'.

That is the limit of tolerance. Once words are enclosed in quotations they should be the words the speaker actually said.

Here is a report as it arrived (left) and as it was edited.

The Town Clerk said: 'The committee reluctantly decided to defer consideration of this request and to ask the owners to meet them to discuss the reasons for, and the implications of, the owner's proposal.'

The Town Clerk said: 'The committee reluctantly decided to ask the owners to meet them to discuss the proposal.'

The meaning has been subtly changed—and the quotation marks are a lie. It is surprising what deskmen, in a rash of confidence, will sometimes do. In another report which appeared a bishop referred to 'a financial crisis in the diocese'. The deskman inserted the word 'grave' in the quotes, reasoning that a crisis must be grave, and then carried the word 'grave' into the heading because church and grave seemed to him apt together. Heresy!

Courts and hospitals Clearly, editing court reports needs especial care (*see* pp. 173–80). But the legal pitfalls do not justify the way police language is reproduced in the majority of humdrum cases in the lower courts. Nor do legal cautions excuse the false gentility of many newspaper reports:

A milling crowd of students followed a *police officer* for *a distance of* a quarter of a mile the night he arrested a fellow student for *causing an alleged* breach of the peace.

Magistrates, who fined the student £5, were told that P.C. Alan Goad arrested him . . .

Three other students, *who were called as witnesses for the defendant, said in court* that the group was orderly.

A milling crowd of students followed a policeman for a quarter of a mile the night he arrested one of them for a breach of the peace.

(*Policeman will do to describe a P.C. —and why 'an alleged breach' when the case is found proved?*)

Three other students said . . .

(*The context makes it clear they were in court. 'Who were called as witnesses' is almost always verbosity.*)

When apprehended Dooney had in his possession two radios.

When stopped Dooney had two radios.

Dennis Bloggs was fined £4 when he admitted behaving in a disorderly manner on a Corporation bus and breaking a bus window.

Dennis Bloggs was fined £4 for being disorderly on a Corporation bus and breaking a window.

County police are anxious to know of his whereabouts.

County police want to find him.

The constable telephoned headquarters and when two officers hurried to the scene they found the youths on the premises of the store.

The constable telephoned headquarters and two officers found the youths in the store.

John Jones was fined £5 for having inefficient brakes on his van and £2 for having an inefficient speedometer.

'*Having*' *is redundant.*

Editing of injuries and hospital conditions is often equally woolly. There should be an office style:

Alfred Davidson received a sprained neck when his car was in collision with a truck . . .

Did he get it in a gift-wrapping?

> Alfred Davidson sprained his neck
> when his car and a truck collided . . .

That is shorter and more direct, but passive reporting predominates:

Sandy Smith suffered a leg injury.	Sandy Smith hurt his leg.
Lawrence Jones was fatally injured.	Lawrence Jones was killed.
Howard M Woods, of 53 Hillside Avenue, was *reported in* a 'fair *condition*' last night at Central Hospital. He has a heart ailment. He was admitted *to the hospital* on June 22nd.	Was 'fair' last night. . . . That is enough. The quotation marks reveal that it is the description of his condition. He was admitted with a heart ailment on June 22. Where else but to the hospital?
He was allowed home after treatment.	He went home after treatment.

A caution: the quotes on a hospital condition can sometimes look silly:

> Mr J Smith, city engineer, is 'ill'
> in hospital with a heart complaint.

The deskman knows that this is the hospital's exact assessment of Mr Smith's condition. But with an ordinary ailment, the quotes round 'ill' read oddly to the ordinary reader—as if there is some doubt about it. 'Ill in hospital' means 'ill in hospital' to the ordinary reader—and the ordinary reader is our customer.

Finally, some other types of needless repetition:

● Unnecessary doubt: A small Renoir painting was reportedly stolen yesterday. The painting was taken from a wall. 'Was stolen' is enough. Is there reason for doubt? We retell facts, not rumour.

● Useless caution: Why keep saying 'It was learned that . . .'? It is no legal protection if the facts are not right. We could say 'it was learned that . . .' before every fact in the paper.

● Statement of nothing: Do we need to say 'Reached for comment, Jones gave no further details'? If we had further details the reader presumes we would give them. And he is prepared to credit us with trying without having the point made at the expense of two lines which could be used by real information. Of course, when someone is criticised it is worth saying 'Mr Jones last night refused to reply'. Even though he has said nothing, his refusal is a positive act—it is part of the news. But why say 'Reached for comment . . .' at all? How else could he say it if he wasn't reached?

4 Watch this Language

To write simply is as difficult as to be good. — SOMERSET MAUGHAM

The previous two chapters have set down a set of conditions to guide the deskman. Negatively, the series of don'ts means rewriting long sentences, complicated sentences, negative sentences, passive sentences, and a succession of sentences of the same structure. It means avoiding complex words, abstract words, and omitting all needless words. Some of this is summed up in an adaptation of an old nursery rhyme:

> If I had a donkey as wouldn't go
> Do you think I'd wallop him, oh No.
> I'd give him some corn and cry out 'Whoa',
> 'Gee up, Neddy'.

which would appear in too many news columns as:

> If I had an ass that refused to proceed,
> Do you suppose that I should castigate him,
> no indeed.
> I should present him with some cereals and
> observe proceed,
> Continue, Edward.

Edward the donkey is a reminder of what the deskman is up against. He has to work fast. He has to recognise Edward as Neddy in disguise. He has to be ready with the better word. The three lists that follow are an attempt to help. They are words that spell waste. All are taken from newspaper reports. The deskman should know the lists thoroughly. They are not exhaustive. He should add to them himself. If he then cultivates an animus to the offending words, there is a good chance they will spring out of the copy; and he will have a substitute already in mind. The busy deskman will have no time to consult his thesaurus or sit and ponder.

The first list gives the bad expressions on the left. They are not all necessarily wrong. Some of them are, but the alternatives on the right are all generally crisper and shorter. They're not synonyms but they frequently express the desired meaning. If no alternative is given the word is simply one to avoid. The second list is of redundancies, and the third of common newspaper clichés.

Wasteful Words

Don't say	Prefer
abrasions and contusions	cuts and bruises
absence of	no
accede to	grant/allow
accommodate	hold/seat
accommodation	rooms, seats, etc.
accordingly	so
acquaint	tell
act as	bad substitute for verb 'to be'
a cut on his ear	a cut ear
adequate bus transportation	enough buses
adjacent to	near
adumbrate	outline/sketch
affluent	rich/well-off
ahead of schedule	early
a large proportion of	many
a man by the name of	named
ameliorate	improve
a percentage of	some
approximately	about
arrangements were in the hands of	arranged by
ascertain	learn
as far as . . . is concerned	as for (but it is better to be direct)
assistance	help/aid
at an early date	soon
attempt	try
at the present time/at present	now
attired in	wore

Don't say	Prefer
best of health	well/healthy
beverage	drink
bid (except at auction)	attempt
bifurcation	division/split
called a halt	stopped
carry out the work	do the work
caused injuries to	injured
centre round	centre on/in
cloudburst	heavy rain
commence, commencement	begin, beginning
compared with	than
concerning	about/on
conflagration	fire
conservative (estimate)	low/cautious
consist of	bad substitute for verb 'to be'
constructed of wood	made of wood/wooden
continue to remain	stay
currently	now
customary	usual
decease	death/die
deceased, defendant	prefer the name
declared redundant	sacked
demise	death
demonstrate	show
dentures	false teeth
described as	called
despite the fact that	although
discontinue	stop
dispatched	sent
donate, contribute	give
donation	gift
draw the attention of	show/remind/point out
dwell	live
edifice	building
endeavour	try
en route	on the way
evince	show

WASTEFUL WORDS contd.

Don't say	Prefer
exceedingly	very
exceeding the speed limit	speeding
expedite	hasten/hurry
expensive	dear
facilitate	ease/help
filled to capacity	full
fissiparous	separatist/breakaway
following (i.e. later in time)	after
freighter	(cargo) ship
from out of the	out of/from
from Nixon's point of view	for Nixon/to Nixon
gained entrance to	got in
gathered together	met
give consideration to	consider
give rise to	cause
hails from	comes from
headache (except literally)	problem, difficulty, puzzle
heretofore	before/until now
hospitalised	went to hospital
illuminated	lit up
implement (verb)	carry out/fulfil/do
implementation	
impossible of discovery	cannot be found
in addition	also
in addition to	besides/as well as/also
in advance of his meeting with . . .	before meeting . . .
in attendance	present/there
incapacitated	(put) out of action
in conjunction with	and/or
in consequence of	because of
inferno	fire

Don't say	Prefer
inform	tell
in isolation	by itself/alone
initiate, institute	begin/start
in many cases/in the case of	often/with (case is an over-worked word)
in order to	to
inquire	ask
in short supply	scarce
in spite of the fact that	despite/although
in succession	running
in the course of	in/during/while
in the direction of	towards
in the event of	in/if
in the field of	in/with
in the majority of instances	mostly
in the vicinity/region/neighbourhood of	about/near/around
in view of the fact that	since
is of the opinion	believes
it cannot be denied that	undeniably
lady	woman, unless Lady is a title
larceny	theft, stealing
leaving much to be desired	unsatisfactory/bad
less expensive	cheaper
local authority	council
made an approach to	approached
made good their escape	escaped
manufacture	make
materialise	happen/come about/appear
maximum	greatest/greatest possible
measure up to	fit, reach, match
merchandise	goods
minimum	least/smallest
miraculous	surprising/unexpected
missive	letter
necessitate	force

WASTEFUL WORDS contd.

Don't say	Prefer
objective	aim
occasioned by	caused by
of the order of	about
one of the purposes	one purpose
one of the reasons	one reason
on account of the fact that/ owing to the fact that	because
on the part of	by
participate	share/take part (in)
pay tribute to	thank/praise
per	should be followed by another Latin word, e.g. per annum, but prefer, *a* year, *a* head, *a* mile, etc.
permanent	lasting
personnel	men/crew/team/workers
peruse	read
petite	
placed under arrest	arrested
posh	
possessed	had
predecease	die before
prior to / preparatory to / previous to	before
probe	
proceed	go
proceeded up	went
production	output
progress to	reach
proliferation	spread
prove beneficial	benefit
provided	if
purchase	buy
put in an appearance	appeared

Don't say	**Prefer**
quit	leave
quiz (verb)	question/ask
red faces (except literally)	embarrassed
regarding	about/on
remunerate	pay
rendered assistance to	helped
request the appropriation of	ask for (more) money/funds
residence	home
resides at	lives at
respecting	about/on
result in	end in. Keep result/resulted in for scores in games
resuscitate	revive
retain his position as	remain
retired for the night	went to bed
shortfall in supplies	shortage
since the particular time	since then
special ceremonies marking the event were held	ceremonies marked the event
stockpile	stock
submitted his resignation	resigned
subsequently	later
subsequent to	after
succeeded in defeating	defeated
succumbed to his injuries	died
sufficient	enough
sufficient consideration	enough thought
summon (except legal summons)	send for
sustained injuries	was hurt
take action on the issue	act
terminate	end
the remains	the body
this day and age	today/nowadays
to date	so far
took into consideration	considered

WASTEFUL WORDS contd.

Don't say	Prefer
took up the cudgels on behalf of	backed, supported
tragedy	
transmit	send
transportation	bus, car, cycle—or transport
the tools they employed	their tools
under active consideration	being considered
under preparation	being prepared
underprivileged	poor/deprived
under the circumstances	in this/that case
utilise	use
valued at	worth
varsity	
venue	
voiced approval	approved
was a witness of	saw
was of the opinion that	believed/thought/said
was suffering from	had
wend one's way	go
when and if	if
which included	including
whole of	all
will be the speaker at	will speak at
with the exception of	except
with the minimum of delay	as soon as possible
with the result that	so that
worked their way	went
W was in collision with Y	W and Y collided (no blame)

Redundancies

These are expressions which the deskman can strike out without offering a terser substitute. Almost always redundant are the phrases: along the lines of, it should be noted that, it is appreciated that . . . In this list of 200 newspaper extracts, the redundancies are set in italic. Deleting them saves space and improves the sentence.

absolute perfection
35 acres *of land*
acute crisis
adequate enough
a distance of
a hearing *to discuss case*
all *of*
all-time record
among the delegates expected *to attend*
an authority *in his own right*
a number of examples
a period of
appear *on the scene*
appear *to be*
appointed *to the post of*
appreciated *in value*
ascend *up*
as compared with
as never before *in the past*
as yet
a team of 12 workmen
at some time *to come*
attach *together*
awkward predicament

best *ever*
blends *in*
blue *coloured* car
bold *and audacious*
broad daylight

chief protagonist
circular *shape*
classified *into classes*
close proximity
collaborate *together*
commented *to the effect* that
commute *to and from*

complete monopoly
completely outplayed
completely untrue
concrete proposals
connect *up/together*
consensus *of opinion*
continue *in existence*
continue *to remain*
co-operate *together*
cost *the sum of*

dates *back* from
definite decision
depreciated *in value*
descend *down*
died *suddenly*
divide *off/up*
doctorate *degree*
downright lie
drink *up/down*
driver *by occupation*
during *the course of*

early *hours*
eat *up*
eliminate *altogether*
enclosed *herewith*
endorse *on the back*
end product/result
end *up*
entirely absent
entirely new departure
entirely spontaneous
entire state/community/congregation
equally *as*
essential condition
ever since
exact counterpart

REDUNDANCIES contd.

face *up to*
falsely fabricated
few *in number*
final completion/upshot/settlement
flatly rejected
follow *after*
for *a period of*
forbid *from*
for *the* making *of*
for *the month of*
for *the purpose of*
foundered *and sank*
fresh beginning
frown *on his face*
full complement of
full satisfaction
funeral obsequies
future prospect

gainfully employed
gather *up/together*
general public
good benefit
grateful thanks

have been *engaged in* producing
have *got*
heard *various* requests
he lost his eye*sight*
he was seen *in the morning* on his
    pre-breakfast walk
he went *in an effort* to determine
hoist *up*
hot water heater
hour of noon
hurry *up*

if *and when*
in abeyance *for the time being*
include *among them*
intents and purposes

inter-personal friendship
in *the city of* Manchester
in *the course of* the operation
in *the process of* building
in the interim *period between*
intolerable *to be borne*
in two years' *time*
invited guest
involved in a car crash
it is interesting to note that

joined *together*
joint co-operation
join *up*
just recently

last *of all*
lend *out*
less essential
link *together*
little sapling
lonely isolation
made *out* of
major breakthrough
may *possibly*
meet *together*
men *who are* unemployed
merge *together*
more preferable
more superior
mutual co-operation

nearly inevitable
necessary requisite
needless to say
need *necessarily*
never *at any time*
new beginning
new creation
new innovation
new recruits

new record
new renovations
new tradition
nobody *else* but
not *at all*
not *generally* available everywhere

old adage
old veterans
one of the last *remaining*
on the occasion when
on *the question of*
original source
over *and done with*
overtake a *slower-moving* vehicle

pay off the debt
pare *down*
partially harmless
passing pedestrian/car
passing phase
past history
patently obvious
peculiar freak
penetrate *into*
periods *of time*
petrol *filling* station
polish *up*
poor state of disrepair
prejudge *in advance*
presence *on the scene*
pressing for *the imposition of* a 30 mph limit
prominent *and leading*
proposed project
protrude *out*

quite empty
quite perfect

radical transformation
raze *to the ground*
recalled *back*

recommended *back*
reduce *down*
regular monthly meetings
repeat *again*
resigned *his position* as
results *so far achieved*
returned *back*
revert *back*
reward *back*
root cause

saved *from his earnings*
seldom *ever*
self-confessed
separate *apart*
serious danger
seriously incline
settle *up*
short *space of* time
sink *down*
skirt *around*
small *in size*
smile *on his face*
spent his *whole* life
staunch supporter
still persists/continues
strangled *to death*
sufficient enough
summoned *to the scene*
sunny *by day*
surgeon *by occupation*
surrounding circumstances

temporary reprieve
the court was asked to decide *as to* whether *or not*
throughout *the whole length and breadth*
to *consume* drink
topped *the* 200 *mark*
total contravention
total extinction
totally destroyed
true facts

REDUNDANCIES contd.

uncommonly strange
unite *together*
universal panacea
usual customs
utterly indestructible

value judgments
vandals *wilfully* broke
violent explosion
vitally necessary

watchful eye
ways *and means*
whether *or not*
whole *of the* country
widow of *the late*
win *out*
worst *ever*

young infant
young teenager

Stale Expressions

Newspapers used to be rank with cliché. Few in the following list survive in the news pages. They lurk more often in sports and features, especially in the form distinguished by an inevitable adjective or adverb (which is one coupled so inevitably with a noun as to have lost any separate life—breathless calm, lively admiration, bewildering variety). Inevitable adjectives and adverbs should be struck out and the noun left to fend for itself. Other stale expressions in the list can generally felled at a stroke, too. But where other words are needed, beware of substituting an over-contrived simile or metaphor just for the sake of brightness.

acid test
aired their troubles
all walks of life
appear on the scene
armed to the teeth
at pains to explain

beat a hasty retreat
bees in his bonnet
beggars description
bewildering variety
bitter end
blaze (for fire)
blazing inferno
blissful ignorance

bolt from the blue
breakneck speed
breakthrough
breathless silence
bring up to date
brook no delay
brutal reminder
brute force
built in safeguard
burning issue

calm before the storm
chequered career
cheered to the echo
cherished belief

city fathers
clean pair of heels
cold collation
colourful scene
commendably patient
concerted move
conspicuous by its absence
cool as a cucumber
coveted trophy
crack troops
crowded to capacity
crude fact
crying need
curate's egg

dame fashion
daring daylight robbery
dark horse
dashed to the rescue
dastardly deed
dazzling sight
deafening crash
deciding factor
deftly manipulate
dig in their heels
ding-dong struggle
doctors fought
dog in the manger
64,000-dollar question
dotted the landscape
dramatic new move
dreaming spires
drew a line

fair sex
fall between two stools
fall on deaf ears
far cry
fickle fortune
filthy lucre
finishing touches
fit and bronzed
fly in the ointment

foregone conclusion
from time immemorial

gay abandon
gay cavalier
getting into full swing
given the green light
glared daggers
goes without saying
gory details
grim reaper

hardy souls
headache (for problem)
heap coals of fire
heartfelt thanks
heart of gold
high dudgeon
hook line and sinker
hook or by crook
hot pursuit
hub of the universe

inextricably linked
in full swing
inspiring/unsporting display
internecine strife
in the nick of time
in the same boat with
in the twinkling of an eye
iron out the difficulty/problem

lashed out
last but not least
last-ditch effort
leaps and bounds
leave no stone unturned
leave severely alone
left up in the air
lending a helping hand
like rats in a trap
limped into port
lock, stock and barrel

STALE EXPRESSIONS contd.

long arm of the law
long years
loom up
lucky few
luxury flat/yacht

mantle of snow
man worthy of his steel
marked contrast
marked improvement
marshal support
matter of life and death
mercy dash
milady
move into high gear

never a dull moment
news leaked out
nipped in the bud
none the worse for wear
not to be outdone
not to put too fine a point on it

official capacity
open secret
order out of chaos
over and above

paid the penalty
painted a grim picture
paramount importance
part and parcel
patience of Job
paying the piper
pillar of the Church
pinpoint the cause
place in the sun
pool of blood
poured scorn
powder keg
pretty kettle of fish

pros and cons
proud heritage
psychological moment

raced/rushed to the scene
raining in sheets
rats in a trap
red faces
red-letter day
red rag to a bull
reduced to matchwood
reins of government
remedy the situation
rose to great heights

sadder but wiser
sea of upturned faces
selling like hot cakes
shackles which fetter
sigh of relief
sons of the soil
spearheading the campaign
speculation was rife
spirited debate
spotlessly white
spotlight the need
square peg in a round hole
staff of life
steaming jungle
stick out like a sore thumb
storm of protest
storm-tossed
stuck to his guns
sweeping changes

taking the bull by the horns
taking the situation in stride
terror-stricken
this day and age
through their paces
throwing a party

tiny tots
tongue in cheek
top-level session
tower of strength
true colours
turned turtle

unconscionably long time
up in arms
upset the apple cart

vanish in thin air
voiced approval

wealth of information
weighty matter
whirlwind tour
widespread anxiety
winds of change
wreak havoc
writing on the wall

5 The Structure of a News Story – Intros

'Under the impression your peregrinations in this metropolis have not as yet been extensive and you might have difficulty in penetrating the arcana of the modern Babylon—in short,' said Mr. Micawber, in a burst of confidence, 'you might lose your way.'
—CHARLES DICKENS

Hemingway, I read once, wrote the last page of *A Farewell to Arms* sixteen times before he was satisfied. It is the beginnings that give newspaper writers all the trouble. One does not want to suggest Hemingway was not trying, but sixteen shots at the first sentence or paragraph of a news story is nothing, as is proved every day by the number of failed first paragraphs screwed into tiny balls on any newsroom floor and the mortality tables of copydesk executives. Any effort to get the beginning right in a newspaper story is worthwhile, because the reader will stop there if the writer fails. What bothers the newsman when he sits down to write his first paragraph (called an 'intro' in Britain and a 'lead' in America) is that it seems to him he is being asked to sum up in one paragraph a drama akin to *King Lear* crossed with *My Fair Lady*. If it is not that kind of story, it is the other kind, the fourteenth report of the sanitation and waterways committee, and everyone knows it is easier to follow *Lear* than the mental workings of a county surveyor committing himself to prose. So despite the constant injunctions for intros to be kept short and to the point, reporters will keep coming up with thoughts impossibly complicated for a newspaper, and deskmen will have to keep putting them right.

Before we get into this quagmire, let us glimpse the kind of solid ground provided by the late Eugene Doane in the *New York Sun*:

> Chicago, Oct. 31: James Wilson
> lighted a cigarette while bathing his
> feet in benzine. He may live.

Eugene Doane's intro is a rare piece. It manages to tell the whole story from beginning to end. That is splendid, but only the brevity is commended for copying. To sum up such a sequence in two sentences is impossible in most stories. Until somebody like James Wilson does it again and somebody like Doane is around to record it, the wise reporter and deskman should concentrate the hard news intro on effects rather than origins, on what happened rather than how, when or where. He should offer a short sharp sentence conveying a maximum of impact in a minimum of phrase. Of course concentrating tersely on effects can be overdone. James Thurber once rebelled and wrote:

Dead. That's what the man was when he was picked up.

The practical aim for newsmen is somewhere between Thurber's cannonball and Doane's epigrammatic essay. An intro as short as 19 words can be inviting:

> The first time 53-year-old Sidney
> Anderson was seen drunk was the
> last time he was seen alive.

That intro from *The Northern Echo* would have been spoiled if an address or a date or a location or the coroner's name had been added. Many offices lay down a maximum number of words for a lead. That sounds primitive, but it is necessary and helpful. It forces the writer to essentials. Where longer intros are tolerated, reporters and deskmen easily drift into writing the comprehensive unselective intro, with grammatical constructions that are invariably confusing.

There is a typographical objection to long intros, too. They look slabby and uninviting to read. It should be possible to read the intro—and digest its meaning—in a quick scanning. If you have to read an intro with care it is a failure.

A 40-word *maximum* would not be at all unreasonable: about 30 words is better. Editors of the spoken word in broadcasting especially should aim for the shorter intro. Long sentences with subsidiary clauses are a snare for announcers and a strain on the listener.

A limit of 30–40 words is not hard to achieve. The skill is in achieving brevity without depriving an intro of precision. Anybody can write a 5-word intro: 'A man was killed yesterday'. That is not news. It is a vacuum. Filling it with just the right amount of detail is where the skill is needed. Too little specific content makes an intro vague; too much is bewildering. The editor has to make sure the intro is precise enough to refer to a unique happening, but the precision must not be prolix. A great deal of harm has been done by the old rule that the intro should try to answer the questions Who? Why? What? Where? When? This is a rule for a news story, but not for an intro. The intro must concentrate on effects, on one news idea. It must contain some identification, but origins, sequence and chronology are all subsidiary to what resulted in the end. The preoccupation with trying to answer all those five questions overloads too many intros, to the detriment of meaning. This obsession with secondary detail manifests itself in a number of ways, but two grammatical symptoms are of prime importance. Where intros begin with a long subsidiary clause or a participle, you are in the presence of a muddle.

In the next example the opening clause is set in italic. All this building material has to be carried along in the mind as meaningless junk until the main clause (from 'materials availability') has been read. Only at the end of the long sentence does the reader know what the intro is all about. Meaning is acquired more quickly if the sentence is turned round (right) to begin with the main clause:

With no sign that there is a general improvement in the supply of common bricks, despite big increases in production, or of copper tubes and fittings and sanitary ware, materials availability remains the building industry's most urgent problem, reports the National Federation of Building Trades Employers.	The National Federation of Building Trades Employers reports that materials availability remains the building industry's most urgent problem, with no sign that there is a general improvement in the supply of common bricks, despite big increases in production, or of copper tubes and fittings and sanitary ware.

But better still, of course, the language should be changed as well as the sentence structure: 'materials availability' and 'building industry' are clumsy abstract ways of describing a simple specific:

> Builders are still being held up by a shortage of common bricks, despite big increases in production, and of copper tubes and fittings and sanitary ware, says the National Federation of Building Trades Employers.

A very common form of opening with a subsidiary clause betrays a split mind:

> While Lord Hill was denying last night that the BBC was considering advertising to offset costs, the head of Scottish Television claimed the Government was threatening the future of ITV.

Behind this intro there is a failure of decision. There are two news ideas. The writer has to make up his mind.

> Lord Hill denied last night that the BBC was considering advertising to offset costs.

> The managing director of Scottish Television, Mr ————, claimed last night that the Government was threatening the future of independent television.

Intros beginning with a participle are similarly weak and muddled. The participle is the weakest part of the verb and it is usually the intro to a long subsidiary clause:

> *Referring* to the statement made on Labour plans to force local authorities to introduce comprehensive schools, Alderman ———— ————, Conservative Leader of the Inner London Education Authority, said: . . .

> *Criticising* the Administration, Senator Muskie last night . . .

> *Saying* that on Friday he had agreed terms for the relief airlift, Colonel Ojukwu yesterday . . .

The subsidiary clause at the beginning of a sentence asks too much of the reader. The first part of the sentence means nothing until he has read the second part. He may give up. If he goes on, he has to hold in his mind the jumble of words until he has read a second jumble of words which then give meaning to the whole. Even the writers of subsidiary clauses themselves lose their way and relate the preamble to the wrong subject:

> Alarmed by the wave of violence that has swept Singapore during the last six months, the death penalty has been passed on those guilty of kidnapping.

> Plump, crew-cut, blinking a little behind black-rimmed spectacles, Allan Sherman was born in Chicago in 1924.

Opening with a subsidiary clause is especially irritating when there is an unidentified pronoun:

> With what his colleagues called a 'clarion call' to party unity, Mr . . .

> Declaring that it could not be opened until officially approved, Mr . . .

Whose colleagues, what party? What could not be opened—a public house, a church, an envelope? No reader should ever be asked to cope with such conundrums.

Finally, trouble can also come from long subsidiary clauses in the middle of an intro. What follows is a newspaper example where the reader has to carry two subsidiary clauses in his head before being told what the fuss is all about. This intro can be rewritten in the active voice (1 below).

That delays mentioning the three baby-food manufacturers, which is a pity, but the words baby-food makers will be in the headline. Alternatively (2 below) the intro can lead off with the baby-food manufacturers and the badly intruding second subsidiary clause (*by the scientists who headed the work that led to the banning of cyclamates*) can be compressed and transposed so that it does not interrupt the flow of thought. The use of a dash in punctuation here gives the reader a pause and the story a neat emphasis.

The three baby-food manufacturers, Heinz, Gerber and Squibb Beechnut, who voluntarily withdrew all monosodium glutamate from their products at the weekend were accused today, by the scientists who headed the work that led to the banning of cyclamates, of panicking unnecessarily, and causing public alarm.

(1) Scientists whose work led to the banning of cyclamates accused the three baby-food manufacturers, Heinz, Gerber and Squibb Beechnut, of causing needless public alarm by the voluntary withdrawal of monosodium glutamate from their products.

OR

(2) The three baby-food manufacturers, Heinz, Gerber, and Squibb Beechnut, who voluntarily withdrew all monosodium glutamate from their products at the weekend, were today accused of causing needless public alarm—by the scientists whose research led to the banning of cyclamates.

Let us now examine in detail the obsessions with secondary news ideas, with chronology, and with source, which produce bad intros.

Chronology

In certain feature and news-feature reports (discussed later) a chronological construction is appropriate. This is a clear narrative technique. It is quite different from allowing secondary details to creep into the hard news intro.

> After hearing shooting at the Berlin Wall yesterday an American military policeman raced to the scene and found East German guards trying to drag a refugee back. The American soldier went to a second-storey window overlooking the Wall, threw a tear-gas grenade, to make the East Germans release the refugee, then climbed on top of the Wall and amid a hail of bullets between East and West helped to pull the refugee to the West.

This is dramatic reading but it is nowhere near good enough for a hard news intro. The antecedents of the action—which have produced a subsidiary clause at the beginning—are secondary. They come unnaturally in the excitement of telling the news. Anyone who had seen that incident would say: 'I saw a tremendous rescue at the Wall today—an American soldier dragged a refugee across. They were shooting at him all the time'. That is the germ of the hard news intro. 'Yes', your listener will say, 'and what happened to the soldier and the refugee? Were they killed?' 'The refugee was wounded but they told me he'd be all right.'

If you had been telling the story chronologically, that piece of information would have had to wait till the very end of a long recital. Your listener (and the reader) would rightly grow very impatient. In conversation and in news reporting one begins naturally with a quick account of the action—and the result. If we do this here we discard the preamble 'after hearing shooting at the Berlin Wall yesterday'. Indeed we discard the whole first sentence. The first attempt now at a hard news intro can be built from the way one would have told the news orally.

> An American soldier dragged a refugee across the Berlin Wall yesterday. The East Germans were shooting all the time. The refugee was wounded but his life is not in danger.

This tells the news but it is staccato and imprecise. It omits the fact that both sides were shooting during the rescue. It sounds routine: journalists would say it is colourless. Try again:

> An American military policeman braved a hail of bullets to pull a wounded refugee over the Berlin Wall yesterday.

This has compressed the action and tells the result. Even in the second paragraph of the lead we would still avoid going right back in the chronology ('after hearing the shooting').

We would cram in some more action, and begin to substantiate and explain the intro in this second paragraph:

> The soldier, 22-year-old Hans Puhl, threw a tear-gas grenade to make East German guards release the refugee. Then amid fire from the East and counter-fire from the West, he climbed on the Wall to drop a rope to the wounded man, Michel Meyer, aged 21.

You will notice how we have saved till later the explanation of how he climbed on the Wall from a second-storey window—and of course how he came to be on the scene at all. These things happened first, but they are not first in importance and so they have no place in the intro. Only now, in the third paragraph, can chronology take over. The men's names have been given in this second paragraph so that the rest of the story can be told more easily without the confusion of two 'he's' or the elegant variations 'the refugee', 'the soldier'.

In a second example below the obsession with chronology has produced a gargantuan subsidiary clause, introduced by a participle. The intro is rewritten on the right with a simple announcement of the statement's effect.

Replying to Viscount Lambton (C. Berwick-upon-Tweed) who asked if the Minister of Agriculture would relax existing restrictions on the importation of live and dead poultry following upon the introduction of the fowl pest vaccination policy, Mr Christopher Soames said in the House of Commons yesterday: 'I have decided, following the recommendations of the Plant Committee, to allow the importation of poultry breeding stock and hatching eggs where this is likely to be of benefit to the commercial stock in this country.'

Poultry breeding stock and hatching eggs may now be imported more freely. The Minister of Agriculture, Mr Christopher Soames, told Viscount Lambton (C. Berwick-upon-Tweed) yesterday that, following the Plant Committee's advice, imports would be allowed where they were likely to benefit our commercial stock.

A chronologically obsessed intro does not always begin with a tell-tale subsidiary clause or participle. In the next example the intro begins directly enough, but its concern with an over-long sequence delays the real human news. The locational details aggravate the failure. 'A field near Chatham Gardens Apartments' does not merely intrude extra words, it delays the action. On the right is the rewritten version—constructed in the same trial and error process as the Berlin Wall intro.

A bulldozer, started up at full speed by vandals and then abandoned, raced one-quarter mile across a field near Chatham Gardens Apartments last night and rammed into a bedroom where two children lay sleeping.

Neither of the children was injured by the six-ton machine which hit a crib containing a two-year-old boy and knocked it several feet across the room.

The vandals, described as teenagers by witnesses, jumped off the out-of-control bulldozer moments before the crash and fled on foot. Damage to the building is expected to run into thousands of dollars.

Patrolman Edgar Bastian and Dominic Rotolo said the two sleeping children were William Gray, 2, and his sister Marguerite, 10 months. Their parents, Mr and Mrs Richard Gray, were not at home.

A runaway six-ton bulldozer rammed into a bedroom where two children were asleep last night. It knocked a crib containing a two-year-old across the room.

But the children were unhurt.

The bulldozer was started at full speed by vandals on a field near . . .

You will note where chronological sequence is allowed to take over—after the news lead.

Source Obsession

This disease gives priority to the event, place, organisation or person that yielded the news and too little to the news itself. Here we might usefully distinguish three rough categories of news intro:

● The general news intro retailing a fact for the general reader. This needs a minimum of source identification: 'Pensions will go up by 25p a week from January 1'. The source for such a plain fact can follow in the second part of the sentence, or in a second sentence. Too often it intrudes into the first sentence and when there are a lot of such details the intro becomes confusing.

● The general news intro retailing an opinion or quote for the general reader. This needs an early statement of source so that the reader can judge the worth of the statement: 'The Prime Minister said yesterday that he believed unemployment would fall "dramatically" in the next three months'. All opinion stories must have the source in the first sentence—but the place and occasion of the statement are subsidiary and can follow in the second.

● The specialist news story retailing either fact or opinion for specialist readers, i.e. for local readers, for business readers, or sports readers, and so on. In sports and business sections of national newspapers and in local newspapers prompt identification is required because the names are the essence of the news: 'Joe Bloggs is "certain" to play for England, said the team manager, Sir Alf Ramsey, yesterday.'

The commonest news stories are in the first category, retailing a fact for the general reader. Here for every quotable individual justifiably edging into the first words of an intro, there are ten of this kind, either plain or fancy:

> It was announced in the *Church Times* yesterday . . .

> At a special meeting of Manchester Corporation Housing Committee this afternoon, it was agreed after a three-hour meeting that . . .

All this before the reader is let into the secret of what the report is all about. Insignificant elements of source in factual general news intros can be deferred to the second paragraph, letting the first sentence tell the news:

> All Manchester Council house rents will go up by 25p a week. This was decided at . . .

The worst defect of source-obsessed intros in all three categories is focusing on the administrative mechanics behind the news—the committee, the bill, the statement, the hall where the meeting was held, the official who distributed the handout:

> North Riding police yesterday issued a statement on the arrangements for the Queen's visit . . .

This makes the issuing of the statement, rather than its content, the important item. There are other examples of how easily the obsession with source makes the administrative mechanics appear to be the news:

> In its voluminous report submitted to the Government earlier this month, the committee on educational integration is understood to have made 213 major recommendations touching upon all aspects of education, including the medium of instruction, education policy and the functioning of universities.
> One of the most important recommendations of the committee is that . . .

This is where the intro should begin—with this precise recommendation. The second paragraph will do to tell the reader it is part of a 'voluminous' (i.e. bulky, or 700-page, or 5½lb) report.

The rewritten version on the right below, bringing the live subject into the news at the earliest moment, saves 3–4 lines of type on a 13-line story:

A bill to authorise the study of the feasibility of keeping the St. Lawrence Seaway open all year round has been approved by the House Public Works Committee.

But the Committee yesterday amended the bill, which had been

Ways are to be sought to keep the St. Lawrence Seaway and Great Lakes open all year round.

The House Public Works Committee yesterday approved a bill to investigate harbour and channel de-icing. But it amended the bill,

passed by the Senate, to limit the cost of the study to a maximum of 50,000 dollars. The study would include ways of de-icing harbours and channels to permit winter navigation.	which passed the Senate, to limit the study to 50,000 dollars.

The next example is an intro from the middle category. The news value of the story depends here on the source, in this case the Law Society, the professional organisation of English solicitors (a description which few text editors handling the agency story bothered to give the reader). The early identification of this authoritative source, however, emphatically does not mean overloading the intro with more than the source, as on the left. The intro should be as on the right:

The Council of the Law Society in a memorandum on motoring offences to the Lord Chancellor, the Home Secretary and the Minister of Transport today, recommends the setting up of traffic courts and special corps to relieve the police of non-criminal traffic commitments.	The Law Society wants traffic courts and special corps to relieve the police of non-criminal traffic duties. In a memorandum today to . . .

It would be wrong to delay a source beyond the intro, or to lead with an unidentified pronoun:

> Traffic courts and special corps to relieve the police of non-criminal traffic commitments are 'urgently required' says a memorandum on motoring offences today.

> They deplore the waste of the police's time on non-criminal traffic offences, says the Law Society today, in calling for traffic courts and a special traffic corps.

No pronoun should ever be used for an intro before the noun is introduced:

He was opposed to capital punishment which he depicted as 'a barbarism that has judicially murdered innocent men', said the leader of the Progressive party, Mr. Snudge.	The leader of the Progressive party, Mr. Snudge, condemned capital punishment yesterday as 'a barbarism that has judicially murdered innocent men'.

Where the source of the statement determines the news value it is best to begin by naming the source at once.

Now, finally, for the third category—the relevance of the newspaper's audience to the amount of source detail in an intro:

> A father was electrocuted yesterday
> as he tried to fix the fairy lights on
> his children's Christmas tree.

That is the essence of the news. It is fine as a general news intro retailing a fact for the general reader of a national newspaper, or a London evening. But imagine the accident happened in a town of 80,000 and the story is being edited for the evening paper. Then the intro could profitably say: 'A Luton father was electrocuted yesterday . . .'

Take it a stage further. The accident happened in a small market town and it is being edited for the town's weekly newspaper. It now becomes a story for a specialised audience. It would now be right to let the intro say: 'Mr . . . of . . . was electrocuted on . . .'

The text editor must ask himself this: How many readers will be induced to read the story primarily by the inclusion in the intro of the name of the man, or place? Is it significant to the readers of this newspaper? On local or provincial papers text editors should err on the side of including the name in the intro. When the area referred to is cheek by jowl with the publishing centre of the paper it looks needlessly vague to write:

> The future of a town's ambitious
> swimming pool scheme hangs in the
> balance after a shock victory last
> night by opponents of the plan.

Readers of that in a Bristol area paper could have been told without fear straight away that it was nearby Keynsham's scheme. The following intro would have been all right in a national paper:

> A managing director under fire from
> housewives who claim his factory
> chimney wrecks their washing has
> asked a local councillor to help
> track down complaints.

But that intro appeared in a Darlington paper and about a Darlington factory. The second paragraph went on:

> Mr D J Grant, head of Darlington
> Chemical and Insulating Co., has
> asked Coun. Clifford Hutchinson

> to join him in ending the washday
> menace of the Faverdale area of the
> town.
>   Last week residents complained
> that grit from the chemical works
> chimney is burning holes in their
> washing.

For the local paper this second paragraph, plus recognisable names and places, would have been better as the intro: indeed the first paragraph could be deleted altogether.

There is a further inducement for the regional newspaper to be more specific (but without falling back on subsidiary clauses). It is that disguising the identity of the place leads to the proliferation of vague intros hinged insecurely on the indefinite article:

> A council chairman has resigned
> because of a row over prayers . . .

> A doctor has accused a local authority of carelessness . . .

Overloading

Details of sequence and source have been identified as two impediments to the intro. The third is trying to make one sentence carry too many details or ideas. That is a fault in a sentence anywhere. In an intro it is fatal. Yet it is a common failing even among sophisticated reporters. Entranced by all he has discovered, the reporter is tempted to thread all the most colourful beads on to the same thin thread of a sentence, and it just breaks.

> Mr Joe Bloggs, the handsome grey-
> haired missing textile company
> founder, aged 48, who had a passion
> for fast sports cars, and was often
> seen with Princess Hilda, the wool
> heiress, before disappearing from
> the Dover Express on July 2, will be
> charged with misappropriating
> £325,086 in the High Court on
> September 1.

Hell, yes, but what size hat does he wear?

That fictional example of Reporters' Baroque is 53 words, at least 20 too long for the basic news. If the text editor works to a word limit he has to strike out the excess detail for insertion lower in the story. This is the real justification for limiting the number of words in an intro. As well as discouraging subsidiary clause openings, it forces the editor to squeeze the real news into the intro. A guillotine concentrates the mind wonderfully.

One simple sentence to an intro, one idea to a sentence. In the example below, the 44-word first intro on the left needs two breaths. The version on the right restricts itself to the single news idea—that a policeman's sense to keep talking saved the lives of a family. Once that single idea has been conveyed in the intro, substantiation can follow:

A policeman kept up a running telephone conversation with a despondent mother of five who said she was going to turn on the gas in her home and end the lives of herself and her children last night, then quickly dispatched a police car.

Police Constable Peter Folino said the woman called twice and said she had turned on the gas on the second call. Then she hung up. Because of Folino's quick action, police arrived in minutes and turned off the gas before the mother or children suffered any ill effects.

She was being questioned early today.

Police Constable Peter Folino kept talking last night—and saved the lives of a mother and five children.

The despondent woman phoned the police to say she was going to gas herself and her children.

Folino talked and quickly sent the police who turned off the gas before the family was hurt.

He said the woman had called twice. On the second call she said she had turned the gas on, then hung up.

She was being questioned today.

The second version saves three lines on a story originally totalling 17 lines: a worthwhile saving for the ten minutes that it should take to write off the more direct version. Notice again the way the story develops in the rewritten version. Only when the intro has established the news point—the happy ending—does the story go back to the beginning of the event and develop chronologically.

The news gets lost again here, and the intro should be split, as on the right, into two sentences:

A noisy meeting of 3,000 workers voted in Birmingham today to instruct their shop stewards to get the BMC management and the ETU together to settle within 24 hours the pay dispute which has halted all car production and thrown more than 21,000 men idle in the Midlands.

A noisy meeting of 3,000 workers voted in Birmingham today for peace moves in the BMC pay dispute which has halted car production and thrown more than 21,000 idle in the Midlands.

They instructed their shop stewards to get the BMC management and the ETU to settle within 24 hours.

Most overloaded intros can be lightened in quick subbing. The facts deleted are then interpolated in the next paragraph or lower. This transposition of a phrase or two can make all the difference to the immediate intelligibility of an intro. The italicised section here does not need to be in the intro:

> A former French parachutist who was serving a life sentence in the island fortress of St Martin de Re *for complicity in the murder of a police officer in the Algiers insurrection of 1962,* has escaped by means which recall the flight of Edmond Dantes from the Chateau d'If in The Count of Monte Cristo.
>
> He is believed to have left the prison, which is about a mile off La Rochelle on the Atlantic Coast, in the trunk of another prisoner pardoned by President de Gaulle and released on Friday evening with two others.
>
> The man, Clause Tenne, was reported present when the morning roll call was taken, though officials are not sure now whether it was he, in fact, who replied 'present'.

The first intro is 55 words long. The literary reference is fine, but the reader loses some of the flavour by the way the editor has left in so much superfluous detail. The italic section should be transposed to the third paragraph or even lower as a separate background statement:

> Tenne was imprisoned for complicity in the murder of a police officer in the Algiers insurrection of 1962.

Editors on copy can, again, save this overloaded intro:

> It is a sobering thought that, ten years after the Committee on Grass Utilisation, *under Sir Sydney Carne,* reported that improved methods in production and use of grass *were not coming into wide use as rapidly as they should,* speakers at a *conference on grass conservation* at Bristol last week should have used even stronger words *to describe the existing situation.*

That really needs rewriting, but quickly editing the intro as it stands the words in italics can be deleted altogether or easily transposed to a later sentence to leave:

> It is a sobering thought that, ten years after the Committee on Grass Utilisation called for better methods of grass production and use, speakers at a conference at Bristol last week should have used even stronger words.

In the discussion so far I have stressed the need to shed the intro of extraneous detail, whether of sequence, source, or subsidiary news point. But clearly the words that remain in an intro must pull their weight. It is easier to keep the intro short if it does not carry identifying detail; but some specific identifying detail is needed in all news intros. The test is whether the detail applies to a single news point, how far it identifies that news subject and how far it merely adds decoration. If the detail is an integral identifying part of a single news point, it is unlikely to be an example of sequence or source obsession or overloading. The intros on the left below show the perils of denuding. They are anaemic compared with the intros with detail on the right. The anaemic intro is a less common error, but it demonstrates the limits of word-shedding and economical generality.

An agricultural show cancelled some events yesterday because of the spread of cattle disease.	All livestock classes at the Royal Smithfield Show were cancelled yesterday because of the spread of foot-and-mouth disease.
An air crash in which British holidaymakers died last month may have been caused by poison gases leaking into the pilots' cabin.	The pilot of the DC4 chartered airliner which plunged into a mountain near Perpignan last month, killing 83 British holidaymakers, was probably seriously affected by carbon monoxide poisoning.

Two Aids to Better Intros

We have now examined three main causes of bad intros: chronology, source obsession and overloading. Before we look at some specialist problems of the intro, here are two suggestions for finding a route through any labyrinth.

The telegram Where does the avalanche of words touch real life? What effect is the news buried in it going to have on people's lives and happiness? Decide that, then imagine telling that news by telegram. Obviously we do not want an intro in telegraphese, but the mental trick often helps to elicit the real meaning of the story: the deskman will find he dispenses with the incidentals, the venue and the background and the tempting details. It is just the same as imagining having to tell somebody urgently what the story is all about. It is gratifying how this simple trick helps to shed literary complications and reveal the hard nugget of news.

For instance, in the following story, exactly as received by teleprinter, the deskman would not dream of *talking* about 'consequential increases'. And anyone would have to think hard if he had to send this message by telegram at £5 a word: that is really the way we should think of the cost of wasting words in a newspaper.

> If British Railways decide to forgo an application to the Transport Tribunal for fares increase in the period for which London Transport have agreed not to make fares increases, any consequential increase in British Railways' revenue deficit will rank for grant, Mr Tom Fraser, Minister of Transport, said in a written answer.

The deskman should think of the telegram being sent to a rather aged relative who wouldn't know a subsidiary clause if it hit him.

BRITISH RAILWAYS INVITED BY TRANSPORT MINISTER FRASER TO PEG FARES FOR SAME PERIOD AS LONDON TRANSPORT STOP GOVERNMENT WILL PAY ANY DEFICIT.

This telegram should then be filled out:

> British Railways were invited to peg their fares yesterday by the Minister of Transport, Mr Fraser. He said that if they agreed to keep their fares down in the period already agreed by London Transport, the Government would meet any deficit.

If the deskman looks at the following intro on an accident story and applies the telegram technique, the clouds disappear. Nobody would tell a friend, 'Minor head lacerations were suffered by Peter Muratore'. One would say 'Peter Muratore fell asleep and crashed . . .'

> Minor head lacerations were suffered by Peter Muratore, 36, of 287 Hartsdale Road, Irondequoit, about 2.45 a.m. yesterday when he fell asleep while driving north in River Boulevard, at the University of Rochester campus, and crashed into a parked car, police said. He was treated at Strong Memorial Hospital and released. The parked car was owned by Mrs Shirley Graham, Greenville, S.C.

PETER MURATORE, 36, 287 HARTSDALE ROAD, IRONDEQUOIT, FELL ASLEEP DRIVING NORTH IN RIVER BOULEVARD STOP CRASHED INTO PARKED CAR UNIVERSITY ROCHESTER CAMPUS 2.45 A.M. MINOR HEAD CUTS TREATED STRONG MEMORIAL HOSPITAL STOP PARKED CAR OWNED BY MRS SHIRLEY GRAHAM.

And we end up with this intro:

> Peter Muratore, 36, of 287 Hartsdale Road, Irondequoit, fell asleep while driving north in River Boulevard and crashed into a parked car at the University of Rochester campus at 2.45 a.m. yesterday.
>
> He was treated for minor head cuts at Strong Memorial Hospital. The parked car was owned by Mrs Shirley Graham, Greenville, S.C.

It is absurd, in any event, to start with such a low-key word as 'minor'. Always look for the positive statement for the intro, and, subject to accuracy, save the qualifying and nullifying statements for a subsidiary position.

The key word   In trying that technique of putting the copy aside and composing a mental telegram, the deskman will often find that a single word or phrase is the vital signal. With the accident to Mr Muratore it was 'fell asleep'. This 'key word' concept is one of the secrets of writing successful headlines (*see* Book Three). It can also help with intros. Here is an example. The Middle East Command in Aden announced

one Saturday that two named soldiers were missing presumed dead
after a clash with rebel Yemen tribesmen. The next day the Army commander called a press conference and announced that the men who had
died in the fighting were later beheaded and their heads were exhibited
on sticks in the Yemeni capital of Taiz.

Now, the news here comes down to a single word: BEHEADED.
The intro has simply to say that two soldiers killed in fighting *were
beheaded*. But look how one morning paper handled the story:

> The heads of two British soldiers
> killed last Thursday were exhibited
> on sticks in Taiz, twin capital of the
> Yemen, according to 'reliable in-
> formation' given to a Press con-
> ference in Aden yesterday by
> Major-General John Cubbon, GOC
> Middle East Land Forces.

The deskman has allowed the second event—the exhibition of the heads
—to overtake the real news which was the actual beheading. Until the
reader has realised that there has been a beheading he is not ready for the
information about heads on sticks in Taiz. The *Daily Mirror* intro was:

> A British officer and a soldier, killed
> in an ambush by the 'Red Wolves'
> of the Yemen, were beheaded by the
> Arabs.
> Then their heads were put on
> show sticks at Taiz, twin capital of
> the Yemen, it was revealed yester-
> day.

The criticism of this intro is that it takes too long to reach the key act and
key word, the beheading. The *Daily Express* intro was cluttered:

> Two British soldiers, killed in bitter
> fighting, were beheaded by scream-
> ing tribesmen who carried the heads
> as trophies across the frontier to
> Yemen.
> Then, according to reports reach-
> ing here today, the heads were
> stuck on spikes and exhibited in the
> main square of Taiz, twin capital of
> the Yemen.

The *Daily Mail* intro benefited by its directness:

> Two British soldiers have been
> killed and decapitated by the
> Yemeni.

The *Northern Echo* also did not use the key word, as we see it, but it squeezed in two strong news points intelligibly:

> Two British soldiers killed in fighting with tribesmen had their heads cut off and exhibited on sticks in Taiz, the Yemen capital.

Special Intro Problems

Intros beginning with quotes and intros based on reported speech need critical attention. They are apt to produce problems of identification and meaning and to be replete with officialese.

Quotes Offices where intros are still set with drop caps usually ban quote intros because of the typographical complications. There is more against them than that. The reader has to do too much work. He has to find out who is speaking and he may prefer to move on. Only for the most startling quote will the average reader feel like making the effort. Few baits of quotation are good enough in this over-fished pond. Often, as here, they merely delay the real news point (left), which is given in the version on the right:

'I have had no row with Mrs Castle, but I am very sad at leaving', said London's Mr Traffic, Sir Alexander Samuels, last night after resigning as honorary chief adviser to Mrs Barbara Castle, the Minister of Transport.	London's Mr Traffic, Sir Alexander Samuels, has resigned as honorary chief adviser on road traffic to Mrs Barbara Castle, the Minister of Transport. He said last night: 'I have had no row with Mrs Castle but I am very sad at leaving.'

Quotes are almost always better *in support of* an opening statement. *The Times* made the right choice here:

> Mr. Ian Smith, the Rhodesian Prime Minister, today accused the United Nations of incredible deceit and hypocrisy over its efforts to smash Rhodesia's self-proclaimed independence.
>
> 'I venture to predict', he said in a New Year television address, 'that there is more justice where the demon Satan reigns than where the United Nations wallows in its sanctimonious hypocrisy.'

The next example shows how an intro grounded on the third person can be more pithy and lively.

> Vice-President Humphrey, speaking today on the 21st anniversary of Sir Winston Churchill's 'Iron Curtain' speech at Fulton, Missouri, predicted that the Iron Curtain could be replaced by the 'Open Door'.

This is comprehensible, attractive and accurate. The third-person intro enables the deskman to contrast the Iron Curtain and the Open Door as the Vice-President did, even though Mr Humphrey did not do so in the style of a newspaper intro. To have begun with a quotation would have involved this:

> 'It is my belief that we stand today upon the threshold of a new era in our relations with the peoples of Europe, a period of new engagement', said Vice-President Humphrey yesterday.
>
> 'Exactly 21 years ago today Winston Churchill spoke the well remembered words "from Stettin in the Baltic to Trieste in the Adriatic, an iron curtain has descended across the Continent".... The Curtain has become increasingly permeable in some places. . . . I do not believe that a realistic settlement of European problems can be achieved without the participation of the United States and Russia. The goals of Western European unity and of Atlantic partnership are not in opposition to the goal of the Open Door. They are the key to that door'.

Three paragraphs are now needed to convey the point of Vice-President Humphrey's address. Quotes in stories like this are best used to substantiate the intro, not to replace it.

Should quote intros be banned altogether? It would be a mistake. There are times where the third-person intro is duller or where the problems of identification are not acute:

> The last words the legendary Cuban guerilla leader, Che Guevara, spoke just before he died were to identify himself and admit that he had failed.

That meets the usual criteria for an intro, but *The Times* man wrote a livelier intro, using a direct quote:

> 'I am Che Guevara, I have failed', were the last words of the legendary Cuban guerilla leader, spoken to Bolivian soldiers just before he died of his wounds early yesterday.

And again:

> The Governor-General of Canada, General Georges Vanier, made a plea for unity yesterday.

It is safe but it is not as good as the direct quote:

> 'I pray God that we all go forward hand in hand. We cannot run the risk of this great country falling into pieces.' These words were part of a plea for unity. . . .

Tenses   Sol Chandler once observed of Australian newspapers, addicted to the past tense and conditional, that it would not surprise him to see any paper's splash on a great event start with: 'Australia had declared war on China, the Prime Minister told the Federal Parliament in Canberra yesterday'.

The past tense (left) is slower and can be confusing (does this passage mean Mr Nixon once believed in a volunteer force but has now changed his mind? No, it does not). The dramatic present (right) should be used for intros and main text:

An all-volunteer armed force was the ideal, said President Nixon in a message to Congress.	An all-volunteer armed force is the ideal, said President Nixon in a message to Congress.

Verbosity   Text editors should always be on the alert when they see intros written by rail officials, clerks of works, or court officers. They are not adept at the job.

> A British Rail official said yesterday that the main-line cancellations were

> an economy move because a suffi-
> cient number of passengers were
> not now using the through train.

He meant that *too few people are using* the through train.

Reported statements from officials, if merely rendered direct into third-person, are a common source of muddled intros (and muddled copy). I said something about third-person reporting earlier (pp. 59–65), but the point for now is that the intro does not have to put into indirect speech every single word the man uttered. The freedom third-person reporting gives is to put the news into simpler words—always provided they convey the sense accurately. It is absurd, in these instances, to seek refuge in direct quotes:

Penn Yan—'The adverse publicity against the village of Penn Yann during the past several weeks in regard to the gross pollution of Seneca Lake was based on mislead-ing information issued by unin-formed sources', Municipal Plant Superintendent Leland A Welker said yesterday . . .	Penn Yan—Tests showed Penn Yan village is not to blame for the gross pollution of Seneca Lake, said Municipal Plant Superinten-dent Leland A Welker yesterday. Mr Welker said the adverse pub-licity was 'based on misleading in-formation by uninformed sources' . . .

That intro (left) was written by Municipal Sewage Plant Superintendent Leland A Welker. Municipal sewage plant superintendents need supervision on intro-writing. The reporter or copy editor has to do the work, and he will not—I hope—allow 'in regard to'. It should have been rewritten as on the right.

Portmanteau intros   I have urged deskmen to concentrate in every intro on the single essential news point. There are a few occasions when they have to fall back on a portmanteau intro:

> The President made a major state-
> ment yesterday on problems in the
> Far East, Germany and the Near
> East.

Most portmanteau intros are as dull as this. But every one, even the occasional lively portmanteau intro, carries a real trap for unwary editors:

> Bribery, violence, anarchy and
> ignorance are dramatically exposed
> in a report to be published tomor-
> row by the Institute of Race Rela-
> tions.

It would be hard to contrive a more arresting portmanteau intro. Tell me more, says the reader. But in the long story which followed there was no single word of violence. Deskmen should always check that the story delivers the goods promised in the intro; with portmanteau intros they should check every promise.

Questions No news intro should start with a question, whether in quotes or reported speech, and still less in any other form. Intros are for telling the reader, not for interrogation.

Abbreviations It is unrealistic not to recognise that certain abbreviations have passed so much into the language that they may safely be used in an intro: TV and UN, and NATO internationally; BBC in Britain; and GOP and CBS in the United States. These are a few examples. There are others. Even so, it is good working practice to avoid abbreviations in intros. Just as in text, they should be spelled out when used first time; and the text editor should never assume that initials which are familiar to him will be familiar to the reader. Excessive use of abbreviations is in any event unsightly.

Delayed intros The discussion has so far concentrated on the straightforward news story where the technique is to bring in at once the human results of the activity. There are times when the point of the intro can be delayed with effect. This is when delaying the news point momentarily can add punch or suspense or emphasise a contrast.

There are any number of gradations of delay in a story. I am referring here only to intros. Some stories are deliberately written so that the punch comes in the last line. Court stories in popular papers especially are written so that the routine hard news point is concealed in a vignette. This is a technique affecting the whole construction of the story and we will examine it in the later chapter on construction. For the moment we remain concerned with the general news intro.

The delayed intro in general news can be as short as waiting to the end of the first sentence. Instead of saying 'Peter Bloggs was recaptured yesterday', it could be:

> Borstal escaper Peter Bloggs went for a swim yesterday—and came face to face with an off-duty policeman in swimming trunks.

The delayed intro is a device for all types of newspaper. The serious *Times* for instance:

> The application form described Oliver Greenhalgh as a rodent operative. Questions on qualifications and experience were ignored. After a payment of £11 a certificate was issued stating that Mr. Greenhalgh had been accepted as a fellow of the English Association of Estate Agents and Valuers.
>
> Oliver Greenhalgh is a cat.

The Times also used a delayed intro to effect in reporting on General de Gaulle's tour of Poland. It would have been possible to report the news in the traditional first sentence—that General de Gaulle was rebuffed by the First Secretary of the Polish Communist Party. *The Times* gave the intro an element of suspense with the final words coming like the pounding of a fist on the table:

> General de Gaulle now has the answer for which he has been waiting since he arrived in Warsaw. It came today, from Mr. Gomulka, the First Secretary of the Polish Communist Party and the 'strong man' of Poland, after his address to the solemn session of the Polish Parliament, the Sejm. The answer was hard, uncompromising, and just barely courteous.

Deskmen should consider using a delayed intro occasionally on a suitable hard news story when the normal construction would read like the intro in every other paper. There was a good opportunity to exploit contrast when Britain's submarine, the Repulse, was launched and went on a mudbank. Instead of simply saying 'Britain's submarine went on a mudbank at the launching yesterday', the deskman might have contrived a delayed intro:

> Shipyard workers cheered. A bottle of home-made elderberry wine, released by Lady Joan Zucherman, broke over the bows. HMS Repulse slid proudly, perfectly down the slipway at Barrow. And two minutes later £55million-worth of Polaris submarine was aground on a mudbank.

To sum up this chapter on intros here is a horrific talisman of 79 words, subsidiary clauses and all:

> In his address to the annual meeting of North Riding Dental Practitioners, held at the Golden Fleece Hotel, Thirsk, the chairman, Mr. C. W. L. Heaton, expressed his concern that there were still many practitioners in the area who did not appreciate the importance of their attendance at meetings as complacency of this nature did not give much encouragement to those who were striving to secure a betterment factor in forthcoming negotiations between the Minister of Health and the dental profession.

6 The Structure of a News Story – The News Lead

The structure of a news story depends both on length and content. The story told in three or four paragraphs is simply an intro followed by further details. As the length increases, however, those further details multiply and their introduction and treatment must be handled carefully. Much will depend on the nature of the story whether it is basically one of action or one of statement and opinion. Chronology is a guide to the construction of the action story: it is no guide to the construction of the complex statement–opinion story.

Action Stories

Let us return to the story of the Berlin Wall rescue (pp. 89–90). The original intro was:

> After hearing shooting at the Berlin Wall yesterday an American military policeman raced to the scene and found East German guards trying to drag a refugee back. The American soldier went to a second-storey window overlooking the Wall, threw a tear-gas grenade to make the East Germans release the refugee, then climbed on top of the Wall and amid a hail of bullets between East and West helped to pull the refugee to the West.

We rewrote that intro:

> An American military policeman braved a hail of bullets to pull a wounded refugee over the Berlin Wall yesterday.

The intro now distills the essence of the news. It is a simple direct sentence not overloaded with detail. But it has not indicated all the most important news points in a long and detailed story. This now has to be done in other sentences and paragraphs which together make a news lead. Each succeeding sentence should be as simple and direct as the intro. It should give a news point and, if possible, add detail the generalised intro has omitted:

> The refugee was hit five times— but he will live. The soldier, 22-year-old Hans Puhl, threw a tear-gas grenade to make East German guards release the refugee. Then amid fire from the East and counter-fire from the West, he climbed on the Wall to drop a rope to the wounded man, Michel Meyer, aged 21.

The most dramatic items of the news story have now been presented in a succinct news lead. Some of the identifying details (such as names) excluded from the intro have been added—but without delaying the development of the key points. The news lead has concentrated on results. It has omitted both other detail and explanation. The story now has to explain how the refugee, Meyer, got into his predicament; how the soldier, Puhl, climbed on the high wall, how he came to be on the scene at all, how the firing started. How should we do all this? In action stories, as I have said, chronology is the master. Once the most dramatic items have been presented—and only then—we go back to the beginnings and build a sequential narrative. In doing this, we check that every point in the news lead is substantiated—for instance that there was a 'hail' of bullets and not merely a couple of shots. The logical narrative is simple enough. The skill is in the way we amplify what we have already told the reader and knit together the two sides of the story.

The paragraph after the news lead should read something like this:

> Meyer had swum the River Spree to reach the Wall at dawn. East Border guards opened fire and he was hit five times in the arm and legs. Hans Puhl, born in Bremerhaven but taken to the US when he was 14, was on duty at the Checkpoint Charlie crossing-point when he heard the shooting about 100 yards away.

We have gone back to the beginning of the action, both for Meyer and Puhl. We have explained how Meyer and Puhl got where they did and have given an anticipatory explanation of Puhl's fluent German. Everything now follows the way it happened, told as much as possible in the words of the actors:

> Puhl, rifle in hand, climbed to a second-storey window overlooking the Wall and saw Meyer being held by two uniformed East Germans who started to drag him away.
>
> 'I pointed my rifle at them and shouted in German: "Let the boy go",' Puhl said. 'When they ignored me I threw a tear-gas bomb. It landed only a yard from them and they let go of Meyer.
>
> 'Two civilians lifted me up and I leaned against the top of the Wall with my hands resting on it. I held my pistol loaded but cocked. I saw Meyer lying there and told him in German: "Stay there while we cut the wire (barbed wire on top of the Wall)".'
>
> Three East German guards in a trench 100 yards away began firing at Puhl, an easy target in his white MP's hat: 'Shots hit the top of the Wall and debris was flying all round me'.
>
> Two West Berliners cut through the barbed wire fencing topping the seven-foot Wall and firemen helped to drag the fence down. Then they threw a rope down to Meyer. All the while bullets were flying in both directions over the Wall, hitting houses on the West Berlin side and damaging furniture in the flats. Meyer fastened a loop of the rope under his arms and was pulled up. On top of the Wall he collapsed and was dragged across by his clothes.
>
> A woman eyewitness in a house by the Wall said: 'It was a terrible scene. The boy never uttered a sound. I could see he was hit and he never screamed. It was eerie'.

This ends the action. Note that quotes are introduced to provide variety and directness; how little use is made of the continuation word 'then'—too many 'thens' make it sound like a police report; and that we have now substantiated the lead without using the same words: 'bullets were flying in both directions' is better than repeating the intro phrase 'hail of bullets'.

Having concluded the action, we can now add non-action background and assessment, which has no part in the chronology (and which could all be cut under pressure of space).

> Puhl said he had been entitled to fire at the East German guards as he was allowed to shoot in defence, but he had not done so.
>
> Yesterday's incident occurred within half-a-mile of a memorial at the Wall to Peter Fechter, the 18-year-old East German boy left to bleed to death at the foot of the Wall in 1962. 'The action by our MP evens the score for Peter Fechter', said one American officer.
>
> It was the longest battle since the Wall went up and the most serious in that it was the first time a US soldier had gone into action to save a refugee.

This then should be the normal construction in action stories:

1. Intro and/or news lead: the most dramatic incident(s), the human result(s) of the activity.

2. Development in chronological narrative.

3. Background and assessment if any.

Here is the story of an award for a pit rescue, with my comments on the right:

Colliery overman Mr John Hodgson, aged 50, of Silksworth, turned himself into a human pit prop when a fall of stones threatened to crush a trapped man at Silksworth mine. For his gallantry he was last night awarded the British Empire Medal —and was amazed by it.

It was a night shift at the Silksworth Mine on January 12, says

Intro: the most dramatic presentation—and the conclusion in two sentences: first the rescue, then the medal, and his reaction.

the *London Gazette* citation. Three men were working on withdrawing waste edge supports. There was a sudden fall of stone from the roof and one of them was trapped. He was pinned in a sitting position behind a conveyor belt drum box, under a fallen roofbar and partly buried by rock.

'Overman Hodgson quickly arrived on the scene and immediately took charge of rescue operations. Realising that great slabs of stone which were hanging over the trapped man would fall if orthodox methods of support were tried, he directed two men to steady them on each side while he himself, sprawled across the drum box, supported the centre.

'Hodgson instructed the others to jump to safety and then he released his hold and scrambled back over the conveyor belt in a working height of only 4ft 6in.

'The whole roof above the place where the man had been trapped immediately collapsed, filling the space where the men had been working to rescue him.'

Mr Hodgson's two colleagues, Mr Walter Appleby, of 50 Potts Street, Sunderland, and Mr Harry Cooper, of 32 Ashdown Road, Sunderland, were both awarded the Queen's Medal for Brave Conduct.

Mr Hodgson, a miner for 30 years, was amazed to hear of his award last night. He recalled being questioned by a mines inspector, but added: 'They seemed to be harping on about it and I thought there might be an inquiry'.

The man trapped by the fall, Mr Ernest King (52), of Holborn Road, Hilton Lane, said last night: 'I have had other lucky escapes since I started at Silksworth in 1937 but I have never been trapped like this.

'It's a queer feeling just lying there with tons of stones likely to fall'.

The action has ended. Supplementary details can now be added.

Backing up intro again.

It would not matter to the construction if these paragraphs were higher, say before the mention of the Queen's Medal. The essential is to tell the action chronologically, substantiating the intro before bothering about other details.

Statement - Opinion Stories

The last action story was simple enough. It did not need a news lead with a sentence for each of a series of key points. And, after the intro, the story had a simple structure based on chronology and given in an excellent original account. Statement–opinion stories are more difficult to construct. News values determine their structure. The beginnings of speeches or documents or inter-related series of verbal exchanges do not begin the news story unless they provide the most important news. Importance, not chronology, is the art of this narrative. The action story requires the most dramatic points in the news lead, with some detail; the statement–opinion story requires the most important points in the news lead, with some detail. The art of the news lead in both types of story, is in picking out all the highlights with just the right amount of detail.

This is a subtle matter. What we shall call the *generalised* news lead indicates the highlights of the story without giving the details. The absence of detail keeps the lead reasonably short; the strength of the generalised lead lies in being comprehensive and intelligible. Its weakness is vagueness. The specific news lead gives details at once. Its strength is precision. Its weakness is that if it is to remain brief it cannot indicate all the highlights of the story; and if it tries to do that it can become too long and confused.

Ideally, in the longer stories there should be a news lead which in three or four sentence/paragraphs summarises every news point with some of the detailed identification. It is not enough, in 100 words of news lead, to give the news points in a wholly generalised way. By the time the reader has read three or four paragraphs he should have begun to find the generalised news points clothed in precise detail. All the points in the headlines should have been covered by this time.

Let us examine a statement–opinion story as it was treated in a number of different newspapers, and consider the ideal blending of the general and the particular in the news lead and deployment of the secondary news points. The story was that the Minister of Technology, Mr Anthony Wedgwood Benn, had attacked the American Westinghouse Corporation for trying to tempt away a team of British atomic scientists. The scientists had been working on two advanced atomic power reactors and in an appeal to the scientists to stay, Mr Benn disclosed that Westinghouse had previously made a 'completely inadequate' offer for a licence to manufacture the reactor.

There are both precise and generalised ways this story can be told in an intro and news lead. Given roughly 100 words the challenge is to construct a news lead which deals with these points:

1. Mr Wedgwood Benn has written an unprecedented open letter appealing to certain British atomic scientists to stay in Britain.
2. He has attacked a US company for trying to tempt them away as a team.
3. This company's bid to manufacture the reactor under licence had previously been rejected because the bid was 'completely inadequate'.
4. This is not, therefore, just another 'brain drain' story. The company was offering salaries three to five times the scientists' present salaries, much more than the normal differential between US and British salaries.
5. Even so, this was an attempt to catch up 'on the cheap' on Britain's world lead in fast-breeder reactors, a lead gained by 20 years of investment by the British people at a cost of hundreds of millions of pounds.
6. Twenty-four Dounreay scientists had replied to the Westinghouse advertisement.

These facts, in an intro and news lead, can be expressed in either a generalised or specific way. The short generalised expression is on the left, the longer specific version on the right.

The Government	Mr Anthony Wedgwood Benn, Minister of Technology.
An American offer	An offer by the Westinghouse Corporation.
Atomic scientists	Atomic energy scientists and engineers at Dounreay, Scotland, and Risley, Lancashire.
Atomic plants	Fast-breeder reactor at Dounreay and design establishment at Risley.
Tempting salaries	Salaries three to five times the present salaries. Westinghouse understood to offer £3,000 to £7,000 for a scientific officer, rising to £15,000 to £35,000 for the best senior staff. Salaries at Dounreay range from £1,100 to £5,000 a year.

An attempt to gain British knowledge	Westinghouse had previously offered to buy a licence for the fast-breeder reactor but offered terms 'completely inadequate in respect of the commercial value'.
An American bid to gain British scientists	Westinghouse advertised and 24 Dounreay scientists have answered the advertisement.

Before reading further, deskmen might try writing a news lead of around 100 words. This will consist of an intro sentence, followed by two or three supporting paragraphs. The news lead must cover all the news points intelligibly and give as much information as possible.

How the Dailies Handled the Story

A good example of a wholly generalised intro appeared in the *Daily Express*:

> The Government last night issued an unprecedented appeal to Britain's leading atomic scientists not to join the brain drain to America.

This intro is vague. It gives no details on the single news point chosen. It does not give any idea of the other news point that a Minister is attacking an American corporation for a particular act of poaching. The story advantage of a generalised intro has therefore been wasted. At the other extreme, the *Daily Telegraph* was specific:

> Mr. Wedgwood Benn, Minister of Technology, has written to atomic scientists working at Dounreay, Caithness, and Risley, Lancashire, warning them of an American plot to discover the secrets of Britain's latest reactor, the fast-breeder reactor at Dounreay, by persuading the senior scientists working on the project to join the Brain Drain.

This intro has tried to indicate the two news points of the appeal to scientists and the attack on an American company but it loses the reader in the particulars. It is 52 words long. It is also going further than strict accuracy would permit in the word 'plot': this was not used by the Minister.

No other daily attempted to indicate these two news points in one sentence. Three of the other dailies chose to concentrate the intro sentence on the news point of the Minister's appeal to scientists; two concentrated on his attack on the American company. Here are the intros, with comments:

Intros angled on the Minister's Appeal

The Minister of Technology, Mr. Anthony Wedgwood Benn, last night took the unprecedented step of writing an open letter to atomic engineers and scientists who have been offered jobs by an American company. *(Sun)*.	More specific than the *Express*, but it fails to indicate the line of Benn's letter or the reason for it.
Mr. Anthony Wedgwood Benn, Minister of Technology, made a dramatic appeal last night to Britain's top nuclear scientists to refuse a tempting offer to join an American firm. *(Daily Mail)*.	More specific than the *Express*. It spells out Benn's appeal to the scientists to refuse and it indicates the news point of high salaries.
Mr. Anthony Wedgwood Benn, the Minister of Technology, last night appealed to Atomic Energy Authority scientists and engineers to resist recruiting efforts by the Westinghouse Electric Corporation of the United States. *(The Times)*.	A specific intro—but by concentrating on a single news point it remains intelligible. It is precise—without following the *Telegraph* too deeply into the woods. Nothing would have been gained in this context by generalised references to 'atomic scientists' or 'an American company'.

Intros angled on the Minister's Attack

Technology Minister Mr. Anthony Wedgwood Benn lashed out last night at an American company's bid to recruit top British nuclear scientists. *(Daily Sketch)*.	Fairly generalised intro but it omits the reason for the Minister's attack —the attempt to get nuclear technology 'on the cheap'.
Mr. Anthony Wedgwood Benn yesterday made an unprecedented attack on a major United States corporation for trying to get British nuclear technology on the cheap. *(The Guardian)*.	Generalised (unlike the intro above it fails to specify Benn's position in the Government). This intro gives the reason for the attack, but does not indicate that the US corporation is trying to recruit British scientists.

The Times intro is the most successful. It is an example of the specific intro at its best—concentrating on a single news point, it is able to be precise without becoming long or confused. None of the generalised intros really succeeds as well because none exploits the opportunity given by the generalised style for indicating more than one highlight of the story. Is it possible in one sentence to cover both the news points of the Minister's attack on the corporation and his appeal to scientists? It is. For instance:

> Mr Anthony Wedgwood Benn, Minister of Technology, appealed to British atomic scientists yesterday not to join an American company which was, he said, trying to gain British nuclear technology on the cheap.

This suffices but it is not wholly satisfactory. It is short enough, but running the two news points together reduces their force, especially as one has to be relegated to a subsidiary clause.

We are in fact dealing with a story which has so many news points and details that a news lead is inescapable. An intro sentence alone cannot cope with the news points and the supporting details. We now examine how the group of British dailies and one American paper coped with the news lead:

The *Telegraph* news lead was:

> Mr. Wedgwood Benn, Minister of Technology, has written to atomic scientists working at Dounreay, Caithness, and Risley, Lancashire, warning them of an American plot to discover the secrets of Britain's latest reactor, the fast-breeder reactor at Dounreay, by persuading the senior scientists working on the project to join the Brain Drain.
>
> Twenty-four atomic scientists from Dounreay, where salaries range from £1,000 to £5,000 a year, are understood to have replied to an advertisement by the Westinghouse electrical company of America, offering jobs in the United States.
>
> Westinghouse offers are understood to be between £3,000 to £7,000 for a scientific officer, rising to £15,000 to £35,000 for the best senior staff.

This is 112 words. It is precise (overlooking the misuse of 'between' in the last par). But it omits the important news point about the inadequate bid for a licence. This is a failing, and the reason for it is that the *Telegraph* spends too many words substantiating the American company's persuasion. The second and third paragraphs are almost wholly devoted to salary details. These should have been dealt with succinctly in a general way ('salaries three-to-five times as great') so that there was space, in the news lead, to bring other important points to the top.

Indeed, this fault continues because the *Telegraph* went on to give details of the Westinghouse advertisement for scientists before telling the reader about the earlier bid for a licence. The *Telegraph* news lead, therefore, is too detailed, to the exclusion of news points.

The *Sketch* news lead was:

> Technology Minister Mr. Anthony Wedgwood Benn lashed out last night at an American company's bid to recruit top British nuclear scientists.
>
> Mr. Benn accused the American Westinghouse Company of trying to cash in on British know-how 'on the cheap'.
>
> And he asked research scientists and engineers in the two major Atomic Energy Authority plants— Dounreay (Scotland) and Risley (Lancashire), to reject the U.S. offers immediately.
>
> The minister's appeal follows Westinghouse pledges of salaries for Britons who join their nuclear power station design plants in Pittsburgh. The money: Up to five times what the men are earning.

This is 97 words. Again, it fails by omitting the central news point about the 'inadequate' bid for a licence. The phrase 'trying to cash in on British know-how on the cheap' is less readily understood—the only comparison given here is in the salaries, and they are not 'on the cheap'. To appreciate the row the reader needs to know about the licence bid, about the attempt to recruit scientists as a team, and the fact that Dounreay has the world's most advanced fast breeder-reactor. If the *Sketch* deskman had added the words 'at salaries three to five times as high' at the end of that first paragraph he could have used the whole fourth paragraph for omitted news points. It is the use of concise phrases like this which enables the deskman to make the news lead really do its work.

Now, the *Daily Express* news lead:

> The Government last night issued an unprecedented appeal to Britain's leading atom scientists not to join the brain drain to America.
> It accused Westinghouse Electrical Company of trying to filch the scientists and their know-how.
> Westinghouse has been advertising for scientists who have been developing the new fast breeder reactor system, on which Britain leads the world.
> The American firm recently made a 'totally inadequate' offer for a licence, Minister of Technology Mr. Anthony Wedgwood Benn, said last night in an open letter to scientists at the atomic energy centres at Dounreay in the far North of Scotland, and Risley in Lancashire.

This is 103 words. The *Express* has recovered from the vague start. The third and fourth paragraphs are concise presentations of news points with details. The licence is there, the 'inadequate' offer, the open letter, Dounreay and Risley, the fast breeder-reactor system, the British lead. Only one news point is missing: the salaries.

The fault with the *Express* news lead lies in those first two pars. It was not really accurate to refer to 'the brain drain' since the Minister stressed this was not a brain drain story. That first sentence could have said:

> The Government last night issued an unprecedented appeal to Britain's leading atom scientists not to let themselves be tempted to America by the Westinghouse Electric Corporation.

This would have freed the second paragraph for a news point. The phrases 'not to join the brain drain to America' and 'trying to filch the scientists and their know-how' waste words on generalities.

The *Sun* news lead was:

> The Minister of Technology, Mr. Anthony Wedgwood Benn, last night took the unprecedented step of writing an open letter to atomic engineers and scientists who have been offered jobs by an American company.
>
> The men work at the Atomic Energy Authority plant in Dounreay, Scotland, where the most advanced power reactor in the world is being built.
>
> America has nothing to compare with Britain's achievement.
>
> Twenty-four Dounreay scientists answered a job advertisement by the American Westinghouse company and some are believed to have been offered posts at up to seven times their present salaries.

This is 95 words. The news points omitted are the licence bid and indeed the whole concept of the Minister's letter as an attack on the American company. Again, the concise way of making the salaries point would have saved space. This could have been done at the end of the first sentence . . . 'at salaries up to seven times higher'. The licence point could then have been brought up from the fifth paragraph (where it appeared) into the fourth paragraph. In the existing fourth paragraph the deskman is led into wasteful repetition: 'The American Westinghouse company' . . . 'Dounreay scientists'. There is repetition in the idea of Britain's lead. The second paragraph at the end says 'the most advanced power reactor in the world'. Then the third paragraph says 'America has nothing to compare with Britain's achievement'. There is no space to spare for this in a pithy news lead.

Look next at the *Daily Mail* news lead:

> Mr. Wedgwood Benn, Minister of Technology, made a dramatic appeal last night to Britain's top nuclear scientists to refuse a tempting offer to join an American firm.
>
> He accused the firm—Westinghouse—of trying to get Britain's nuclear power know-how on the cheap.
>
> The appeal was made in an open letter from Mr. Wedgwood Benn to

Atomic Energy Authority engineers and scientists at Risley, Lancashire, and at Dounreay, Scotland.

The world's most advanced commercial prototype 'fast breeder' power reactor, able to generate electricity cheaper than any other method, is being built at Dounreay. And most of the AEA design work for fast reactors is carried out at Risley.

This is 109 words. The point about the licence is omitted. The salaries above the normal US differential are covered—adequately enough for the news lead—with the 'tempting offer' phrase. All the main news points would have been included if only the licence reference had been added to the second paragraph. This would have squeezed the details about Risley out of the news lead, but that would not have mattered. The *Mail* news lead made intelligent use of general and precise references until the particularisation was overdone with the details of Dounreay and Risley. *The Times* news lead was:

Mr. Wedgwood Benn, the Minister of Technology, last night appealed to Atomic Energy Authority scientists and engineers to resist recruiting efforts by the Westinghouse Electric Corporation of the United States.

He accused the Americans of trying to get nuclear energy know-how on the cheap by offering inflated salaries to attract men away from Dounreay and Risley. He said that Westinghouse had applied to buy the licence for the A.E.A. design of fast breeder reactor some time ago, but had offered unacceptable terms.

In an open letter to the A.E.A. men, Mr. Benn says the A.E.A. is now building at Dounreay the most advanced commercial prototype power reactor in the world—the fast breeder.

This is 114 words—and every one carries its weight. There is no wasteful repetition. There is very little generality—just enough to enable to news points to be squeezed in. 'Inflated salaries' will do for the pay.

'Unacceptable terms' suffices for the Minister's reference to the licence, though 'completely inadequate terms' would have given extra precision for one more word.

Finally for the British papers *The Guardian* news lead:

> Mr. Anthony Wedgwood Benn yesterday made an unprecedented attack on a major United States corporation for trying to get British nuclear technology on the cheap.
>
> The Minister of Technology was appealing to nuclear scientists at the Dounreay fast breeder reactor in Caithness, 24 of whom are thought to have answered an advertisement from the Westinghouse Corporation which would offer them between three and seven times their present salaries.
>
> Mr. Benn wrote that the Dounreay reactor was the climax of 20 years of investment by the British people and that an offer made earlier by Westinghouse was 'completely inadequate in respect of the commercial value of what we have to offer'.

This is 110 words. It vies with *The Times* as the best news lead. *The Guardian*'s generalised intro is sharp. It has the point about 24 men replying to the advertisement and the detail on salary comparisons. *The Times*, however, gains where it is more precise. *The Guardian* omits the key word 'licence' in the third paragraph. It does not really explain that the American company wanted to build the British design on licence. The reference to the Dounreay reactor being the climax of 20 years' British investment almost meets the point about Britain's lead in design—but not quite. *The Times* again is specific here. The news lead in *The Times* is in admittedly quieter vein than some of the others. There are no adjectives. But the language is simple, well chosen, and lets the news make its own impact.

An American Example

This is a story of strong Anglo-American interest. We can now examine the way the *New York Times–Herald Tribune* international edition handled it, in a UPI'dispatch. The news lead was:

The Westinghouse Electric Corporation of America found itself in the middle of a furore today about the brain drain of scientific talent from Britain. A headline in the Daily Telegraph said 'US plot to win British scientists'.

Westinghouse itself in a statement issued in New York and London did not deny it hoped to attract skilled technicians in nuclear research. It said it acted in a 'straightforward manner' in advertising in the British press to fill jobs in the US.

A Laborite MP said he would demand an explanation from Minister of Technology, Mr Wedgwood Benn, who provoked the furore by accusing Westinghouse of trying to obtain nuclear know-how on the cheap.

This is 113 words. There are many things wrong with this as a news lead for American (or British) readers; and indeed the whole story is weak. For American readers the stress on the American company is right for the intro. It is in the further paragraphs that the story fails. The biggest flaw is that the news lead stumbles over itself to give the company's reply before the reader knows what is Mr Benn's central charge. That comes in paragraph 3; paragraph 2 has been devoted entirely to the disclaimer (in the development of the story this is taken up again in paragraph 5). It is far too slow to delay until paragraph 3 that the controversy has been provoked by the British Government. The *Telegraph* headline is colourful and worth quoting but it cannot displace the substance of the story which is that the Minister of Technology has made an attack.

The rest of the *New York Times–Herald Tribune* story was:

He said, in an open letter to scientists at the Dounreay experimental establishment in Scotland, that Westinghouse's offer of employment was not really another example of the familiar brain drain. He said it was instead because of Westinghouse trying to purchase the knowledge and experience a whole team of scientists had gained by hiring away a few key persons.

In reply Westinghouse said many of the scientists involved had education and experience that could be utilised in the company's fast growing nuclear power activities. Laborite, Mr Hector Hughes, said he would ask Mr Wedgwood Benn to tell Parliament how many scientists have gone to the US in the last six months.

Anyone editing this story on an American paper ought not to have been satisfied with it. Why, the deskman might ask, should a big American corporation want British scientists? (Not until the last paragraph is the reader even told that it has something to do with nuclear power for domestic purposes.) Of course the story completely fails to deal with the

Westinghouse licence bid. It fails again by being too generalised. We have 'nuclear research; nuclear know-how; nuclear power' but not once do we have the specific fact that Dounreay is a fast-breeder reactor and a crisp explanation of what that is.

The *New York Times–Herald Tribune* news lead has other faults. The salary comparison is omitted—at least as interesting to American readers as British. And a good deal of space has been wasted by loose wording, some of which is in italics here: '*in the middle of* a furore'; 'scientific *talent*'; 'Westinghouse *itself*'; 'in a statement *issued* in'; 'Westinghouse's offer *of employment*'; '*in reply*'; 'the scientists *involved*'.

So much for the news lead. How should the rest of the story have been developed? There are two immediate necessities. the content of the Minister's letter, so that the remarks can be seen in context and so that the news lead can be substantiated. And, secondly, any reply from the US company. What else? Comments from the atomic scientists involved; comparisons of salaries; discussions of the fast-breeder reactor; and an independent assessment of Britain's position. Having constructed the news lead, the deskman may have to weave these other elements into a composite story from several reporters, the wire agencies, the scientific correspondent, and so on.

There is no set formula for the development of such a news story, only guide-lines. The first is: Substantiate the news lead. The second: Never run ahead of the reader's knowledge. The third: Remember it is your newspaper's job to report the news impartially. Let us see how these guide-lines might have helped us with the atomic scientists story.

Substantiating the news lead means, if possible, running the Minister's letter in full. What if there is not the space to do both this and give the Westinghouse comment plus an explanation of what a fast-breeder reactor is? The other two principles must claim some space and the Minister's letter will have to be cut—or any wordier sections rendered carefully into more concise reported speech.

If we are to take the reader with us into the story, the second principle means that the explanation of a fast-breeder reactor must come fairly high up in the story—before we have used lots of words about fast-breeder reactors on the false assumption that the reader knows already. This explanation need not be long.

The London *Daily Express* did it neatly within parentheses: 'The fast breeder system (by which the nuclear power station makes its own fuel at the same time as it makes its own electricity) is the climax of 20 years of investment by the British people in civil nuclear technology, said the Minister'.

Note the way the explanation is not allowed to delay the development of the story. The same sentence takes the story a stage further. A viable construction here, then, would be:

1. News lead on selected key points, 3–4 paragraphs.
2. Paragraph giving Westinghouse denial (which was brief).
3. Quick explanation in passing of 'fast-breeder reactor' and on into
4. The Minister's letter.
5. Comments from atomic scientists.
6. Scientific assessment of Britain's position; comparative salaries.

Arguably the brief Westinghouse comment could have followed at the end of or adjacent to the story—with a separate headline for prominence. But this treatment requires a certain length. Where denial or comment is brief and the story itself is long, it is unfair to tack the denial at the end, almost as an afterthought. Even if there is a separate denial story a skilled editor should be able to indicate the fact in the main narrative without delaying its progress:

> The Minister's charge—strongly denied last night by the company—was that . . .

The suggested structure for this story makes one assumption: that as section 4 one would choose to publish the Minister's letter in full and certainly in sequence. With a relatively short letter like this no deskman should do otherwise. For the intro it is right to take a striking quote or passage from anywhere in the letter, but later that quote must be given in its proper context (just as intro quotes from speeches should always later be given in context). There is no point in transposing paragraphs at this stage; it is a form of inaccuracy or deception. If parts of the letter are being omitted this should be indicated by sequential dots, or by explanatory phrases for each quotation such as 'The Minister went on . . . He appealed . . . The Minister ended . . .' This is only necessary as a signal to the reader when parts are being omitted. When a document is being quoted in full, it should be allowed to run without such interruptions.

Speeches and Reports

The way speeches and documents may be summarised in third-person reporting has been already discussed (in Chapter 3). Here we are concerned only with the construction of such stories.

They should not begin with the beginnings of the speech or the document unless these beginnings provide the most important news point. They rarely do. News leads on official reports are more likely to be based on points from the conclusions; intros on speeches more often pick up a point from the end than from the beginning. It is common political practice to serve the plums for dessert.

The structure of a speech report should be:

1. Intro stating most important news point, with or without supporting direct quotation in a sentence or a phrase.

2. Any further points summarised in third person with or without incidental quotation.

3. Substantiation of the news lead (1 and 2 above) with direct quotations. This is the only place where third-person reporting needs to be substantiated by production of the direct quotation on which it is based. Any phrases quoted in the intro must also be put in proper context.

4. Development of the speech, preferably of the most important section in direct quotation.

5. Third-person summary of other main points, with or without direct quotes, each to be more briefly treated than the main points.

Judging importance in speeches and statement is, of course, something the deskman can do only with experience and knowledge—knowledge of the subject of the speech, the political context, the news background. There are some general guides. Preference for the intro should be to those parts of the speech which promise or imply action. Opinion and logical argument are not normally as newsworthy as announcements or promises or hints of action. 'Action' is the Prime Minister announcing a proposed new law or the president of a golf club promising to resist a new road across the links. Both are news developments. Something has happened or may happen. There is an attitude which will have repercussions. The deskman must not hesitate to rewrite a reporter's intro entirely if he thinks an 'action' news point is too far down in the speech. He must be ready to do to the report what the reporter has done to the speaker. He must be ready to bring the news point to the top. This was an intro:

> Mr Nikita Kruschev, the Soviet
> Prime Minister, is of the view that
> the provocative flight of the Ameri-
> can reconnaisance plane was only
> a probe and not a preparation for
> war.

But the real news was in the third paragraph of the reporter's copy:

> Mr Kruschev warned that if the
> United States wanted to unleash a
> war 'we shall be compelled to fire
> rockets which will explode bombs
> on the aggressor's territory in the
> very first minute'.

This was the news. It was positive; it implied action. There is a rough test, too, for the newsworthiness of the opinion sections of a speech. It is not enough to say that controversial opinions are news. They may be; or they may be stale. A better indicator of the news value of opinion is the test of contrariness. How much would it surprise you if the speaker were saying the opposite?

If it would surprise you a great deal, there is *no* news value in his present affirmation. There is a report of a speech in which Fidel Castro denounces United States imperialism. That is controversial—but it is not news. If he had praised the United States one would be very surprised. So would the reader. Therefore these latest unsurprising opinions are not worth thrusting on him. An Arab politician says the Israelis are to blame for tension in the Middle East. It would surprise one a great deal if he had said the Arabs were to blame. There is therefore little or no news value in these latest opinions. They are controversial—but they are also predictable. The test of contrariness is obvious, but it is surprising how often it can help if it is addressed to an apparently important, but really worthless, statement.

Running Statement - Opinion Stories

The deskman on a daily newspaper will have often to pull together a series of stories from several sources, arriving at different times, and produce one coherent narrative. The construction is similar to that of the single opinion–statement story, but the deskman must link the separate sections smoothly and interpolate background. This is real subbing. The lazy way is simply to add each separate element of the story as it arrives with no attempt at reassessing priorities. This is a classic example from the London *Times*:

The Supreme National Defence Council of Greece met urgently tonight under the chairmanship of King Constantine after renewed Turkish threats of an impending invasion in Cyprus. The meeting, the second in 24 hours, continued until the early hours of the morning.

A Greek Government statement late tonight said that, if Turkey attacked Cyprus—ostensibly to protect the Turkish Cypriot minority— 'no one would be in a position to avert the automatic exacerbation of the situation on the island, and of justifiable but catastrophic reprisals against the Turkish minority by uncontrollable Greek Cypriots'.

Mr. Pipinelis, the Greek Foreign Minister, said at a press conference that Greece was determined to accept no settlement of the Cyprus dispute which would be 'incompatible with the national interest and Greek dignity'. He said that the Greek reply to last Friday's Turkish Note had been delivered to Ankara. It made suggestions for a settlement of the crisis.

The Turkish Note—which demanded among other things the withdrawal of the Greek troops stationed in Cyprus—was not an ultimatum, he added.

ATHENS, Nov. 22—The Greek Armed Forces were brought to an advanced state of readiness. Military airfields were blacked out throughout Greece and pilots were briefed. Heavy troop movements were reported in north-east Greece, near the Greece-Turkey border. Military movements were also reported on the Turkish side of the border.

ANKARA—The Turkish Cabinet met to consider what one Minister described as Greece's 'rejection' of Friday's Note.

In Istanbul earlier in the day 80,000 demonstrators, organized by students, marched through the streets demanding war.

NEW YORK—U Thant, the United Nations Secretary-General, said he was sending a special representative to Cyprus, Greece and Turkey, to ask the Governments to exercise the utmost restraint and to try to reduce tension.

Mr. Cyrus Vance, a former Pentagon official, left for Ankara as President Johnson's special representative. He will fly on to Athens.

NICOSIA—Turkish reconnaissance aircraft were sighted over Cyprus for the second successive day. One newspaper reported a resignation offer by General Grivas, the commander of the Cyprus armed forces.

LONDON—The situation was described during the day as 'most dangerous'. It was believed that there was a real danger of a Turkish invasion of Cyprus.

The reader lurches through this story with no clear idea where he is going or what is going on. It is left to the last paragraph for at least someone's guidance that the crisis really is considered dangerous. What the deskman has to do is give the reader a God's eye view of the crisis. He has to relate the events in one capital to the events in another. He has to introduce assessment and background and action where they help the reader's understanding and carry the story forward. The same events were presented in this way (author's numerals) in another daily:

1 As 80,000 Turks marched through Istanbul yesterday calling for war with Greece, U Thant, the United Nations Secretary-General, issued an appeal for peace.

2 He announced that he would send a personal representative to Nicosia, Athens, and Ankara, to discuss the situation with the three Governments.

3 At the same time a concerted diplomatic initiative by the American, British, and Canadian Governments got under way. The three countries are to make representations to Greece, Turkey, and Cyprus, calling for urgent action to prevent deterioration in the situation.

4 Behind this is a formula evolved by the Canadian Government earlier this month. Mr. Pearson, the Canadian Prime Minister, who is now in London, had long talks yesterday with Mr. Wilson and the Commonwealth Secretary, Mr. Thomson, on the Cyprus situation.

5 Mr. Pearson thinks that the British and Canadian Governments, by virtue of their troop contributions, supported by American diplomatic power, should be able to insist on far-reaching changes in the present contorted domestic political situation in Cyprus itself. An essential element in this is the personal trust which President Makarios feels for Mr. Pearson.

6 If the UN force were temporarily increased in size and given wider powers, so Mr. Pearson argues, then the Greek and Turkish national forces stationed on the island could be reduced from their present inflated levels of more than 8,000 and 1,000 respectively.

7 It is recognised in London that the danger of Turkish military intervention in Cyprus has definitely grown in the past 48 hours. In Cyprus itself tension mounted yesterday as Turkish reconnaissance planes were sighted over the island for the second successive day.

8 According to diplomatic quarters, there has been a full preliminary deployment of Turkish land, sea and air forces, while the Turkish Government has authorised the President to use far-reaching emergency powers. In the summer of 1964 the two Turkish Houses of Parliament gave the President

authority to order military action in, or in the neighbourhood of, Cyprus. The President has now been authorised to order similar action 'in other areas'—meaning against the Greek mainland or Greek islands.

9 Turkey's militant mood was indicated by yesterday's march in Istanbul while other big demonstrations are planned for today throughout the country in support of the Turkish Government's demands that the number of Greek troops in Cyprus should be drastically reduced, that General Grivas should be dismissed, and that guarantees for the safety of the Turkish-Cypriot minority should be given.

10 In particular, Turkey will continue to insist that there should be no repetition of last week's attacks on members of the Turkish minority by Greek militia and Greek-Cypriot forces. The Turkish suspicion is that these attacks were inspired by General Grivas, in his desire to have a military showdown which could lead to the union of Cyprus with Greece.

11 The British Government is making contingency plans for the possible withdrawal, in the event of large-scale fighting, of British forces on the island to the British sovereign bases. British civilians would, it is assumed, be collected there too. There are about one thousand British troops on the island, and Britain's is the biggest contingent in the UN peacekeeping force. With its Canadian, Danish, Swedish and Irish contingents, the UN force amounts to about 4,500 men in all.

It is worth studying this treatment for its strengths and weaknesses. This is a running story. The crisis was a Turkish threat to invade Cyprus, the Mediterranean island close to Turkey. Behind this threat was a complaint of the Turkish minority on the island that they had been intimidated by the Greek community. A reader knowing none of this should still have been able to understand the story and relate the latest developments to his new knowledge.

First, the structure of this story, then the criticisms.

Paragraphs 1, 2, 3 are the news lead, summarising developments in Turkey, the United Nations, the United States, Canada and Britain. Paragraph 1 is the intro proper. It succeeds in setting the scene for war and the efforts for peace.

The action of the Turks marching through Istanbul adds urgency to the U Thant talks and takes the reader forward, the diplomatic developments beginning in paragraph 2. The scene is changed neatly in paragraph 3 with the transitional phrase 'At the same time . . .'

Paragraphs 4, 5 and 6 elaborate the diplomatic activity and introduce background on the Greek and Turkish national forces on Cyprus. 'Behind this . . .' clearly introduces this phase of the story which is told in three paragraphs.

Paragraph 7 introduces new points—the military activity and the London assessment, and mentions the background threat of a Turkish invasion of Cyprus. It does this smoothly in a way which will tell new readers what the fuss is all about without delaying the story too much for the informed reader:

> 7 It is recognised in London that the danger of Turkish military intervention in Cyprus has definitely grown in the last 48 hours.

Imagine for a moment how much weaker paragraph 7 would have been if the sub had left in the muffling word 'situation':

> 7 It is recognised in London that the situation has definitely grown more dangerous in the last 48 hours . . .

Paragraph 8 substantiates paragraph 7 on the dangers. It leads easily to paragraph 9 with the phrase 'Turkey's militant mood', and there is an inferential reference to the lead intro. Paragraph 10 begins with the signal phrase that detail is to be presented: 'In particular'. It also provides the very necessary background to the genesis of the crisis, the serious omission in the other daily paper's treatment, given earlier.

Paragraph 11 rounds off the story with the specifically British involvement—first the news about the contingency plans, then the background to make them intelligible.

This is altogether a more coherent and meaningful way to handle a story from several sources. Unlike the other treatment it does not assume that the reader has kept in close touch with the story from its beginning. The running news story is not very different from a feature series. The reader needs to be reminded, incidentally, of the story so far.

But even this structure is not ideal. How would you improve it?

There is one thing wrong with the news lead: it does not have the key background words 'Turkish invasion of Cyprus'. The opportunity is missed twice with retreat into the vague tag 'the situation'. The second criticism of the subbing of this story is that it descends to detail and background too quickly, thus delaying important active news. It is not until the seventh paragraph that the military activity is mentioned and the tension on Cyprus itself. This is part of the latest news and worth a place in the news lead. The existing news lead spends too much time detailing the diplomatic activity. *Indicating* that there is intense diplomatic activity is proper for the news lead—but *elaborating* it before other important hard news is wrong.

The solution to all these weaknesses lies in paragraph 7. It is in the wrong place. Transpose it to paragraph 3. This brings in the military news and it does something else: it brings in the key concept of a threatened Turkish invasion of Cyprus. This makes other small textual changes necessary in the subbing. The old paragraph 3 would become paragraph 4. It would be necessary to reword it to refer back to U Thant's activity:

> 4 America, Britain and Canada supported U Thant's peace moves with a concerted diplomatic initiative. . . .

Paragraph 8 would also be affected since it was linked to the old paragraph 7. The sub would have to write a new link phrase to indicate that a new section was beginning at the end of the diplomatic background.

> 8 The urgency of the diplomatic moves was reinforced by reports of a full preliminary deployment of Turkish land, sea and air forces. The Turkish Government has authorised the President. . . .'

Here now is the full revised version:

> As 80,000 Turks marched through Istanbul yesterday calling for war with Greece, U Thant, the United

Nations Secretary-General, issued an appeal for peace.

He announced that he would send a personal representative to Nicosia, Athens, and Ankara, to discuss the situation with the three Governments.

It is recognised in London that the danger of Turkish military intervention in Cyprus has definitely grown in the past 48 hours. In Cyprus itself tension mounted yesterday as Turkish reconnaissance planes were sighted over the island for the second successive day.

America, Britain and Canada supported U Thant's peace move with a concerted diplomatic initiative. They are to make representations to Greece, Turkey, and Cyprus, calling for urgent action to prevent deterioration in the situation.

Behind this is a formula evolved by the Canadian Government earlier this month. Mr. Pearson, the Canadian Prime Minister, who is now in London, had long talks yesterday with Mr. Wilson and the Commonwealth Secretary, Mr. Thomson, on the Cyprus situation.

Mr. Pearson thinks that the British and Canadian Governments, by virtue of their troop contributions, supported by American diplomatic power, should be able to insist on far-reaching changes in the present contorted domestic political situation in Cyprus itself. An essential element in this is the personal trust which President Makarios feels for Mr. Pearson.

If the UN force were temporarily increased in size and given wider powers, so Mr. Pearson argues, then the Greek and Turkish national forces stationed on the island could be reduced from their present inflated levels of more than 8,000 and 1,000 respectively.

The urgency of the diplomatic moves was reinforced by reports of a full preliminary deployment of Turkish land, sea and air forces. The Turkish Government has authorised the President to use far-reaching emergency powers. In the summer of 1964 the two Turkish Houses of Parliament gave the President authority to order military action in, or in the neighbourhood of, Cyprus. The President has now been authorised to order similar action 'in other areas'—meaning against the Greek mainland or Greek islands.

Turkey's militant mood was indicated by yesterday's march in Istanbul while other big demonstrations are planned for today throughout the country in support of the Turkish Government's demands that the number of Greek troops in Cyprus should be drastically reduced, that General Grivas should be dismissed, and that guarantees for the safety of the Turkish Cypriot minority should be given.

In particular, Turkey will continue to insist that there should be no repetition of last week's attacks on members of the Turkish minority by Greek militia and Greek-Cypriot forces. The Turkish suspicion is that these attacks were inspired by General Grivas, in his desire to have a military showdown which could lead to the union of Cyprus with Greece.

The British Government is making contingency plans for the possible withdrawal, in the event of large-scale fighting, of British forces on the island to the British sovereign bases. British civilians would, it is assumed, be collected there too. There are about one thousand British troops on the island, and Britain's is the biggest contingent in the UN peacekeeping force. With its Canadian, Danish, Swedish and Irish contingents, the UN force amounts to about 4,500 men in all.

It would be a good exercise for a deskman to imagine he has to cut this story. He should now have the various elements clearly in his mind. Should all the sections stay and the detailing be reduced? Or should some sections be cut altogether, retaining the other details? In a large international story like this it seems a pity to cut any of the sections: but if this means detail has to be cut it must not be detail which gives the story meaning. Safe detailed cuts (to the full revised version): the second sentence of paragraph 8, and the last two sentences of the final paragraph of the story. The Turkish Government's demands could be confined to the particular demands in paragraph 10, which would save the latter half of paragraph 9. If further cuts were needed the whole of the last paragraph could go. If a really drastic cut were called for, the first four paragraphs would stand—when paragraph 7 of the original story has been transposed. This illustrates again how important it was to move that paragraph higher.

Let us now see how to pull together a series of separate reports on the diplomatic and military moves during the India–Pakistan war. Looking at a typical day, there are agency messages from Moscow, New Delhi, Karachi, Washington and London.

The military reports do not seem to take the war much further, but there is intense diplomatic activity. The two elements which strike the deskman as most newsworthy—and he will have kept himself well informed on developments—are a warning by Russia to China not to interfere and a possible trip to Moscow by the UN Secretary-General. America also warns China to keep out of the war. The deskman would put the messages in front of him and on separate copy paper write off a news lead:

1 Both Russia and the United States warned China to keep out of the Indo-Pakistan war last night. Russia's warning came at the end of a day of intense diplomatic activity and a report that U Thant was on his way to Moscow to seek Russia's help in arranging a cease fire.

Note how crisply news points are compressed into this intro lead— Russia's warning; America's warning; diplomatic activity; U Thant's trip and its purpose.

2 On the battlefront meanwhile India and Pakistan held grimly to their lines in the week-old war, with no sign of a breakthrough by either side.

The news lead continues with an assessment of agency reports from both fronts. The fighting details can now be left until very much later.

3 The Soviet Government's warning to China was in a statement issued

The first four words indicate that development of the lead is about to

by the Tass news agency. It again called on India and Pakistan to stop fighting.and on other nations for restraint and responsibility.

4 China was not named directly but the language pointed unmistakeably to Peking: China has sided violently with Pakistan and condemned Russia's earlier appeals for restraint.

take place. It is substantiation, not repetition.

A key paragraph of background and interpretation written in by the deskman. Running the Russian statement before this interpretation, or worse still without it, would confuse the reader. He would be puzzled by the absence of a specific reference to China.

5 'The whole world and all states', said the statement, 'should warn those who facilitate the fanning of the conflict by their policy that they thereby assume grave responsibility for such a policy and for such actions.

Agency copy. Direct quotes are essential to substantiate the intro and give the tone of the Russian message. At this point the deskman has picked up original agency copy from Moscow and edited that.

6 'No Government has any right to add fuel to the flames. There are forces which seek to profit by worsened Indo-Pakistan relations. By their incendiary statements they push them towards further aggravation of the military conflict—and can cause present developments to escalate into an even bigger conflagration. Many states find themselves drawn into conflict one by one.

Still direct editing on Moscow agency copy.

'This is a dangerous prospect. As shown by the experience of history, this may have the gravest consequences, not only for the peoples of the region where the conflict began, but also far beyond it.'

7 The statement renewed the offer of Russia's good offices in ending the war. After a ceasefire India and Pakistani forces should return to the Kashmir dividing line of the 1949 armistice.

A summary of the rest of the statement written by the deskman.

8 In Washington yesterday, America's warning was given by US Secretary of State, Mr Dean Rusk: 'Our own advice to Peking', he said, 'would be to stay out and let the Security Council settle it'. Mr Rusk said the Soviet attitude had been helpful so far.

The first two words written on to agency copy warn the reader that a new phase of the story is about to be dealt with. The phrase 'America's warning . . .' refers inferentially to the intro and proceeds to substantiate it.

9 [The Chinese have cited Russian appeals for restraint as evidence

Another piece of background information interpolated by the desk-

that Moscow 'revisionists' are working hand in hand with American imperialists.]

10 U Thant's possible trip to Moscow was reported by 'informed sources' quoted by Reuter in Delhi. They said he was expected to fly to Moscow tomorrow. U Thant was in New Delhi yesterday and talked to Indian Foreign Minister Swaran Singh. A second meeting with the Prime Minister, Mr Shastri, was postponed until today.

11 In a big tank battle for the Pakistani town of Sialkot, near the Kashmir border, India claimed her troops had made some advances but Pakistan said the Indians had been beaten back.

On the central front near Lahore, similar claims and counter-claims were made. On the southernmost front Pakistan claimed to have occupied a major part of Indian territory.

India said her troops had thrust further into Pakistani Kashmir.

Pakistani planes reported setting two Indian air bases on fire, raided military installations at three other towns and for the first time struck at Jammu airport inside Kashmir.

man to emphasise the unusual nature of the US–USSR diplomatic agreement and of China's belligerent isolation.

Again the inferential reference back to the intro and then its elaboration. Editing on agency copy.

The story is rounded off with the war reports, the deskman's distillation of a flood of copy.

Caution and compression are the watchwords on a dull day. Claim and counter-claim are related in each instance. It is vital to retain the sources and the contradictions in stories like this. They should not be deleted for space or smoothness. One may be editing out the truth.

The way this story has been constructed should make quick cuts very simple. If hard cutting is needed, the last three paragraphs could go, leaving the reader to survive on the intro indication that the war is at a stalemate. The Soviet statement could be run shorter by deleting paragraph 7, and one element of background could be discarded—the square brackets of Section 9. Paragraph 4 would be retained. If further cuts still were needed the statement could be reduced simply to paragraph 5.

Even while editing a story to a required length a deskman often finds, especially on a busy evening, that further cuts are needed. If he has in his mind a clear structure for the story he will know what is useful but inessential decoration and what sections can be taken away without demolishing the whole house.

7 Background

Background for Intelligibility

It is clear that there are two main tasks for the deskman handling the developing statement–opinion story: getting the structure right, and making the story meaningful to the new reader by writing in background. Of course in a simple story from a single source the deskman can expect the reporter to write the background. Often a reporter fails to do so because he forgets he is a specialist in news. He forgets that while he has been immersing himself in one story the reader has been mending the roads, or auditing accounts, or singing grand opera, or otherwise failing to prepare himself for reading the reporter's complicated conclusions.

Many deskmen make the similar mistake of regarding the reader as a professional digester of everything the paper has ever printed on the subject. In Britain in particular deskmen seem unable to appreciate that the reader may not have been even reading the precious newspaper at all for days. This does not mean retelling the history of the Vietnam War, or reminding the reader that the Berlin Wall was built by the East Germans to separate East Berlin from West Berlin. There are certain landmarks in history like this on which the newspaper has to assume knowledge; but they are far fewer than the average deskman supposes.

In the developing story of a few days' duration, or a foreign story, it is wiser to assume that the reader is a suburban Rip Van Winkle who has slept through all the developments now so familiar to the deskman who has been in the thick of them. The skill is in editing for him without weighing him down with a recital of everything that has been going on. Every developing story has to be constructed so that the vital background information is conveyed but conveyed without unduly delaying the new developments, and without irritating the reader who is up to date.

There is one caution before we see if this can be done: developing court stories are special. The nature of the case must briefly be given, but previous statements by witnesses can be recalled only if they are vital to an understanding of the present proceedings. A background paragraph quoting what a previous witness said (or the same witness said earlier) might be construed as comment. It may well be transparent that the man is not saying what he said when you edited his previous statement. But leave that discovery to the judge and jury.

Background should be given succinctly, in passing. There is no need to recapitulate every single one of the previous facts—just sufficient to make the new developments meaningful. Reporters who have absorbed the idea that background is important sometimes get carried away and present the reader with an unnecessary wodge of yesterday's news. Here are two bad examples from newspapers. The original story is in the left-hand column and my rewritten version on the right.

County Durham club chief, Mr Bob Blythe, yesterday picked up the gauntlet thrown down publicly, he said, by Mr Stan Hall, long-serving secretary of the working men's club movement who has resigned.

It was last week that 43-year-old Mr Hall, who ends his 20 year service with the county Club and Institute Union at the end of next month, said that among his reasons for resigning was that the Northern Federation Brewery Ltd. was 'dictating' to the county's 322 clubs.

He also said there had been a clash of personalities between him, Mr Blythe, president of the County branch CIU, and Mr John Ward, the vice-President.

Mr Blythe and Mr Ward are also two of the nine members on the board of directors of the Federation, the brewery which supplies most clubs in the North with beer and has advanced mortgages for new premises of up to £4½m.

Last week Mr Hall said: 'In spite of the fact that I was clearly employed as secretary of the Durham branch, control was, in fact, exercised by members of the Federation Brewery. Clubs are shareholders and prominent clubmen serve on the board'.

Mr Blythe yesterday said he regretted that Mr Hall had said

County Durham club chief Mr Bob Blythe yesterday rebutted the charges of the former secretary, Mr Stan Hall, that the Northern Federation Brewery Ltd was dictating to the county's 322 clubs.

Mr Blythe, a brewery director as well as president of the county branch of the working men's clubs, said there was 'no feud' between the clubs and the brewery which supplies most clubs and has advanced mortgages for new premises up to £4½m.

Mr Blythe said he regretted etc. . . .

anything about his resignation and was anxious to point out that 'there is no feud existing between the branch executive and the board of directors of the Northern Clubs Federation Brewery.'

The first and last paragraphs are the news: all the rest is background. Some of that background may be required in the story—but later. To begin with, only enough is required to make the latest developments meaningful to a new reader. Other background should be introduced as the narrative progresses.

In the next instance the news is delayed with background in the second, third and fourth sentences. Note the way, in the right-hand rewrite, the 'monstrously noisy' quote has been brought up from the meeting report, and how the end of the intro recaps in nine words' the gist of the first story's second paragraph.

Blanktown urban council, vocally supported last night by some of the citizens, is determined not to let the lorry parking row die down.

Last month the county council voted to take no action on Blanktown's demand that planning permission for the park should be revoked. Blanktown had complained that the County Council should never have passed the plans because the lorry park is built in a once quiet residential area and had brought many complaints locally.

Blanktown has so far organised a petition and had two angry public meetings and last night the anger had not abated. Mr James Johnson who lives two houses away from the lorry park said it was 'monstrously noisy' . . .

[More speeches with a last paragraph:]

The meeting decided to invite the MP to a protest demonstration; to press the County Council and send it full details of complaints; and formally to complain to the Ministry of Housing.

Blanktown urban council, vocally supported last night by an angry meeting of citizens, is determined not to give in over the 'monstrously noisy' lorry park built in a once quiet residential area.

A public meeting sponsored by the Council decided to invite Blanktown's MP to a protest demonstration; to send individual complaints to the County Council, which has refused to revoke planning permission for the lorry park; and to protest formally to the Ministry of Housing.

[Pick up report of the meeting.]

If you are in doubt about where and how to introduce the background, remember that we learn by relating new facts to what we already know. In an ordinary running news story a good general guide is (*a*) give the informed reader a signal in the intro—a passing reference to the news context, and (*b*) give the fuller background, in one paragraph, at paragraph three.

> Sir Basil Blackwell, the bookseller and publisher, told a jury at the Central Criminal Court yesterday that it was nonsense to say that the controversial American novel, *Last Exit to Brooklyn*, was in the tradition of Zola, Dickens and Galsworthy.
>
> Sir Basil, who is 78, was appearing for the Crown to rebut literary authorities called by the defence. He said he considered the literary merit of *Last Exit to Brooklyn* to be slight.
>
> Calder and Boyars Ltd have pleaded Not Guilty to two charges under the Obscene Publications Act, 1959, which allege that they had in their possession copies of the book for publication for gain and that they published an obscene article, namely *Last Exit to Brooklyn*, written by Hubert Selby, jnr.
>
> In reply to Mr John Mathew, for the Crown, Sir Basil said: 'Dickens was a great artist. He certainly portrayed wicked and evil men but he made them live.'

Here the clue in the intro is 'the controversial American novel, *Last Exit to Brooklyn*'. Paragraph 2 takes the story forward by explaining why Sir Basil was there and that he considered the book's literary merit slight. Paragraph 3 is the full background. Paragraph 4 picks up the news events again. Putting the full background in paragraph 3—provided it is restricted to one paragraph—runs little risk of delaying the new events too much. And with a signal in paragraph 1 the reader can be sure of reaching paragraph 3 without perplexity.

You can often indicate the background with a key word in a passing phrase. A report referred to the possibility that the Russians might release an American pilot named Powers. The deskman assumed everybody knew who Powers was. But it is better to tell ten readers, glancingly, what they know than to omit telling one reader the only fact which enables him to understand the story at all. Here the deskman could have played safe by saying: 'Captain Powers, the pilot of the U2 spy plane shot down over Russia . . .' The key reminder is U2 spy plane. Similarly, in this extract the key words are 'border dispute':

> Violence flared when about 5,000 people, protesting against the recommendations of a Government commission on an 11-year-old border dispute between Maharashtra and Mysore states, tried to prevent Mr Y B Chavan, the Home Minister, from attending the meeting.

Background is easier than interpretation; on interpretation you run the risk of introducing too much opinion or bias. This report on a stage in a teaching dispute is essential interpretation:

> After three months during which the National Union of Teachers have been imposing sanctions in more than 1,200 schools, it is clear that its dispute with the local education authorities has reached a climax.

This usefully seizes the reader to say: Look we know you have lost track of all the troubles the last three months, but you really ought to read this latest development.

Interpretation drifts too far when a deskman writes in:

> The Turks *have caused the trouble* by pressing for a drastic revision of the balance of power in Cyprus.

In a bitterly contested dispute, it is enough to say:

> The Turks are pressing for a drastic revision of the balance of power in Cyprus.

If there is one thing the American newspaperman has learned better than his colleagues elsewhere it is the importance of explaining as he goes along. Consider the way Anthony Lewis of the *New York Times* cleverly etches the background for US readers in his report from Britain. The italics are mine to show the phrase written in as background to the events:

> LONDON, Nov. 29 (NYT)—In a major shift of power within the Labor Government and a move toward new policies, Roy Jenkins today became Britain's Chancellor of the Exchequer.
>
> He replaced James Callaghan whose three year struggle to maintain the value of the pound ended 11 days ago in devaluation. Mr Callaghan resigned and shifted to Mr Jenkins's former post as Home Secretary, *in charge of police and other internal affairs.*

The British deskman would not write in copy for British readers the phrase 'in charge of police and other internal affairs'. But he would write in what the US newspaper might leave out when presented with copy referring to, say, Mr Sargent Shriver as director of the Office of Economic Opportunity. He would write in the phrase 'which administers America's anti-poverty programme'. If he does not know that, he should ask for the library clippings, or *Keesing's Contemporary Archives* and the *Statesman's Year Book.*

In domestic stories the biggest failure to provide background or interpretation is in dealing with labour disputes. It may seem that the dispute has dragged on long enough for everybody to know what it is about; but do not believe it. Fair reporting, to both sides, requires that some explanation should be written into every story. And only day-by-day recapitulation saves a reader from being lost in the eddies of negotiation and compromise. The background can be a phrase:

> The drivers, *working to rule because they refuse to have guards riding in freight trains,* are hoping the Trades Union Congress will intervene.

It may be a paragraph:

> The dispute stems from a battle between the Associated Society of Locomotive Engineers and Firemen (ASLEF) and the National Union of Railwaymen (NUR), to which guards belong. The ASLEF drivers fear they will commit industrial suicide if they allow guards to ride in the engine cab now that the freight guards' brake van has been abolished.

It may seem that the longer the dispute goes on, the more the desk-man can rely on a phrase. This is wrong. The newspaper may manage on phrases for a few days, but from time to time a fuller explanation should be written in. This is in the public interest in the wider sense—to enable readers not merely to follow the story but to form their own judgment on rights and wrongs as the labour dispute produces effects on everyday life.

In a complicated dispute lasting several weeks it is a good idea to spend time preparing a concise explanation which can be carried daily in a panel or footnote. Where one or other side in the dispute wants to say nothing, it is as well to record this fact so that your paper is not accused of reporting only one side.

Before we examine how professional deskmen tackled a common problem in a second-day story, one final word on kindness to the reader: don't rub his nose in a scatter of unexplained initials. When the report says the NLF, the deskman should write in 'the National Liberation Front, political arm of the Vietcong . . .' This does not offend the reader who knows and it helps the rest, which is most of us. There was at one time, anyway, another NLF—in Aden—and at another an FLN, in Algeria and France. The way the deskman should deal with organisa-tions and initials is to write out the name in full at first with the initials in brackets and thereafter use the initials:

> Twenty-one members of the Front for the Liberation of Occupied South Yemen (Flosy) who were whisked out of the country at their own request and 10 supporters of the National Liberation Front (NLF) . . .

Of course we have to use judgment in how much interpolation we do. We can get away with UN; but not OECD. (If you do not know what OECD is, your general reading, as a deskman, has some way to go. May it remind you of your need to keep constantly abreast of affairs and improve your general knowledge by consistent reading of the daily and weekly press.)

Having set the standards, let us see how the daily papers managed on the second day of that story in Chapter 6 about the atomic scientists being tempted to America's Westinghouse Electric Corporation. The development announced was that the Minister of Technology, Mr Wedgwood Benn, was flying to the Atomic Energy plant at Risley in

Lancashire and would meet some of the scientists who had been invited to the United States.

In editing this story we have to remind the reader of Mr Wedgwood Benn's vehement protest at the alleged poaching by Westinghouse. We have to do that quite soon in the story so that the significance of Mr Benn's trip is clear: the details of the trip should not begin before Mr Benn's visit has been set in its new context. There is no justification for assuming every reader will recall the news context. We do not need to elaborate it. A concise signal will do.

You might yourself at this point write in one paragraph how you would relay the background. The essential points you want to remind the reader about are: (*a*) Mr Benn is meeting scientists who have been invited by Westinghouse to the United States; (*b*) Mr Benn yesterday condemned the invitation; (*c*) Mr Benn accused the American company of trying to gain British nuclear knowledge 'on the cheap' after underbidding for the rights to it under a proper licensing agreement. To get all three background points in quickly and concisely without delaying the new story requires careful attention to every word.

The Times front page conveyed two of the background points—but rather too late in the story:

> Mr. Wedgwood Benn, Minister of Technology, has asked to meet a delegation of four senior Dounreay nuclear scientists at Risley, Lancashire, tomorrow.
>
> Two of the team of four, representing the scientific staff at the Dounreay research establishment, Caithness, are Mr. Arthur Parry, deputy director of the establishment, and Mr. Roy Matthews, head of administration.
>
> They will fly to Manchester in an aircraft chartered by the Ministry.
>
> Mr. Wedgwood Benn's visit to Risley, one of the two centres of fast-breeder research, is a routine one. But it is understood that it has been brought forward because of the Ministry's concern over the Westinghouse Electric Corporation's attempt to attract nuclear scientists to the United States.

A great improvement is made if the deskman transposes paragraph 4 to be paragraph 2. The existing paragraph 2 links into the new arrangement with a small change of phrasing: ('Two of the team of four Mr. Benn will meet are Mr. Arthur Parry, deputy director of the establishment, and Mr. Roy Matthews, head of administration, who will represent the scientific staff at the Dounreay research establishment, Caithness'). The omission in the background paragraph (4) is Mr. Benn's letter. His strong personal feelings could at least have been indicated if the deskman had changed 'Ministry's concern' to 'Minister's concern'. *The Times* had a much better background paragraph in a story inside the paper:

> Mr. Wedgwood Benn's letter, disclosed on Wednesday, appealed to scientists not to accept the offer and accused Westinghouse of trying to get hold of our information 'on the cheap' after their attempt to secure a proper licensing agreement had failed.

The *Express* gave a clue to the news context in the intro and the background in paragraph 3. Like *The Times*, the *Express* page-one background fails to indicate Mr Benn's personal involvement and does not mention his attack on Westinghouse:

> Technology Minister Mr. Wedgwood Benn will today meet 250 scientists at the atomic energy centre at Risley, Lancs, to discuss the brain drain.
>
> Ten scientists from the Dounreay fast breeder reactor station in Caithness will also be at the meeting.
>
> Mr. Benn's visit was scheduled for after Christmas but has been brought forward, his Ministry said last night, 'in view of the news that Westinghouse are inviting our scientists to apply for posts in the United States'.

The *Express* slips up here by relying on the Ministry spokesmen for the background briefing in paragraph 3. The good thing about the *Express* treatment was the attempt to indicate the background in a phrase in the intro sentence, which could then be elaborated a little later.

The *Sun* had the same technique, but did it much better because the *Sun*'s intro reference gave the reader a clue at once to Mr Benn's passionate involvement '. . . in his campaign to plug the threatened brain drain to America':

> The Minister of Technology, Mr. Anthony Wedgwood Benn, has called a meeting with atom scientists today, in his campaign to plug the threatened brain drain to America.
>
> Mr. Benn will fly to the Atomic Energy Authority Centre at Risley, Lancs, to address 250 scientists and engineers, including a party being flown from Dounreay atomic station in Scotland.
>
> The visit is one of a series Mr. Benn is making to atom stations, but he has brought it forward following reports that 24 Dounreay men have answered advertisements for jobs with the American Westinghouse company.
>
> On Wednesday Mr. Benn published an open letter to scientists at Risley and Dounreay accusing Westinghouse of trying to get British scientific knowledge 'on the cheap'.

The trouble with the *Sun's* development of the background in paragraphs 3 and 4 is that it spends just a bit too much time on yesterday's news: the background is not succinct enough. The deskman would have improved the speed here if in paragraph 4, for instance, he had cut out the words 'published an open letter to scientists at Risley and Dounreay' and simply left it at 'On Wednesday Mr Benn accused . . .'

The *Telegraph* gains full marks for bringing in the background as soon as the second paragraph, but the paragraph is much too vague:

> Mr. Wedgwood Benn, Minister of Technology, is flying north today to visit the headquarters of the Atomic Energy Authority at Risley, Lancs. Arrangements for the visit have been made at short notice.
>
> Yesterday it was disclosed that he has written to atomic scientists working at Dounreay, Caithness and Risley, warning them of an American plot to discover the secrets of Britain's latest reactor by recruiting senior scientists.

The reader might well wonder what 'American plot'? The deskman should have written in a phrase such as: '. . . warning them of an attempt by America's Westinghouse Corporation . . .'

The *Telegraph* itself, in another story, gave a better demonstration of putting the news in context. This was a story of the Westinghouse denial: the denial is the news and in a brief story like this the background should not be too obtrusive. Note particularly how the background is run into the story with the second paragraph phrase 'the company's present recruiting efforts':

Complaints by Mr. Wedgwood Benn, Minister of Technology, that the Westinghouse Electric Corporation was trying to obtain 'on the cheap' the secrets of the Dounreay fast-breeder reactor were firmly denied today by the company.

A Westinghouse spokesman in Pittsburgh said Mr. Benn's interpretation of the company's present recruiting efforts in Britain was 'completely false'. He also said the British Atomic Energy Authority had been demanding a 'completely prohibitive' price for the licensing of information on the Dounreay fast-breeder reactor.

The company refused to say what it had offered Britain in the unsuccessful negotiations to work out a licensing agreement. But it was learned from a reliable source that the parties were '10 million dollars apart' at the end of the talks.

None of these editing attempts was perfect—but they all made an attempt in perhaps hectic circumstances. I have made these criticisms, in more relaxed circumstances, to try to define the aims and standards all good deskmen set themselves. Provided it is accurate, it is far better to make a hurried and imperfect attempt at putting the news in context than not doing it at all. Curiously, the *Guardian*, which did so well on the first day of the Benn story, did particularly badly on the second day —simply by not bothering at all with background. You should sharpen your pencil on this one—the italics are mine and so are the comments on the right:

Mr. Anthony Wedgwood Benn, Minister of Technology, has asked to meet a delegation of four senior Dounreay scientists at Risley today to discuss *the Westinghouse offer*.

What Westinghouse offer? There is not a clue here that it was an offer to recruit individual scientists. Conceivably it might have been an offer from Westinghouse to the British Government. Nowhere in the story is this ambiguity directly resolved.

Two of the delegation will be Mr. Arthur Parry, deputy director at Dounreay, and Mr. Kenneth W. Matthews, head of administration there. They will fly to Ringway, Manchester, in a plane supplied by the Ministry of Technology.

Late last night, Mr. Matthews said: 'Quite frankly, we don't know precisely what's on the agenda for discussion. All we have been told is that Mr. Wedgwood Benn has asked to meet us in Risley tomorrow. But it is a fair assumption that the main topic will be about *the Westinghouse offer.*'

The other members of the delegation are Mr. Kenneth Butler, chairman of the Dounreay branch of the Institute of Professional Civil Servants, and Mr. Geoffrey James, the branch councillor of the institute's Dounreay branch.

Last night a spokesman for the local branch of the institute said that the two officials would point out to the Minister that the reason *why top scientists were wanting to leave Dounreay* was that they did not have the full confidence in their future with the Atomic Energy Authority there.

A deputation from the IPCS which saw Mr. Wedgwood Benn yesterday, told him that there had been prolonged uncertainty over the AEA's research programme. *Dr. Dickson Mabon's* statement about a rundown at Dounreay had never been satisfactorily explained, there had been a severe cutdown at the *world-famous Culham laboratory* and only yesterday staff at *Winfrith* had been warned of a $3\frac{1}{2}$ per cent cut involving 70 people.

There had been an 'extra-ordinary downgrading' of the chairman of the AEA which was in marked contrast with Steel Board salaries and what was being rumoured for the new chairman of British Rail.

Mr. Roy Matthews, director of the Dounreay Atomic Station, from

The reader, as well as Mr. Matthews, is still in the dark.

Properly 'Institution'.

Forget for a moment the clumsy 'were wanting to'. The way this is put suggests that the initiative 'to leave Dounreay' has come from the scientists. The whole story is growing more confusing because of the failure of the deskman to recap on the Westinghouse advertisement and Mr Benn's attack.

And who is he?

Is it really?
Where's that?

which at least a dozen scientists are thought to have been interviewed by the US Westinghouse Corporation, said there was no comparison between Dounreay facilities and Westinghouse, whose fast breeder reactor was only on paper. Westinghouse would be building a prototype when Britain's first commercial fast reactor came into use in the seventies.

For the first time we are told that Westinghouse is an American firm. Even now we are given only a woolly idea that part of the story is about Britain's lead in the fast-breeder reactor and Westinghouse's attempt to catch up.

But there are mixed feelings among the Dounreay scientists. While Mr. Jim Mockett, assistant manager of the reactor, said a recent American visitor from the Enrico Fermi atom station near Chicago was envious of Dounreay facilities, Mr. M. Tucker, a young scientist, said there were a lot of other young men who would like to cross the Atlantic.

'Some of us have been discussing *this advert* and we came to the conclusion we would need about four times our present salary before it would be worth going,' he said.

Which advert?

Westinghouse's nuclear reactor division, based at Pittsburg, has not yet issued any statement following *the row*. A spokesman for the firm in London could not say how many men had been interviewed nor confirm or deny reports of offers as high as seven times their present salaries.

What row? Not a clue that it is an attack by the Minister on Westinghouse. Indeed the *Guardian* seems to have two rows going, since most of the story has been about scientists' criticisms of Government atomic policy.

'But talking in terms of *enticement and underhand activities is absolutely rubbish*', said the spokesman. 'Westinghouse are stretched on the ordinary nuclear power programme—14 projects this year. They have now a fast breeder reactor to produce. They are advertising in the States for men. They know scientists are here, so they placed the advertisement.'

The plot thickens. Who is 'talking in terms of enticement and underhand activities'? There is nothing at all to link this with the Minister. The rest of the paragraph seems irrelevant unless the reader knows of Mr Benn's charge that it was an attempt by Westinghouse to gain nuclear secrets on the cheap.

There are 300 professional people at Dounreay, and the establishment has been reduced in the past year by under 8 per cent, said the spokesman. He did not think the rate of contraction was greatly accelerated during the past year than previously.

He thought morale at the plant was 'reasonably good'. No higher than that? He replied: 'In the early days, when the place was building up, one got a kick out of the freedom and creative activity. We have now gone on to more or less routine work. But on the development side there is still zeal.'

In the Commons yesterday, Conservative MPs pressed for information about what the Government was doing to halt the brain drain. Mr. Peter Shore told Mr. Cranley Onslow (Con. Woking) that no money had been spent by the Department of Economic Affairs in analysing or attempting to reverse the brain drain. 'I would not myself have placed so great a weight on the fiscal system as you do', said Mr. Shore.

Mr Benn's own attempts to halt the brain drain have still not been mentioned: even at this stage Mr Benn's visit to Risley is not projected as an attempt to persuade the scientists to stay in Britain.

Several days after Mr Benn's original letter, *The Sunday Times* took the story further. It provides a useful illustration of the way to give the background while taking the story forward in a piece of informed reporting. Note how in every sentence the background reference is used as a link to new information, thus informing the new reader without wasting the time of the reader who remembers the events earlier in the week:

The attack last week by Mr Wedgwood Benn, Minister of Technology, on the American Westinghouse Electric Corporation was far more than a melodramatic appeal to British nuclear scientists to stay at home.

His impassioned open letter to scientists at Dounreay, Risley, and other centres of fast reactor technology, came only two days after the Prime Minister announced a seven-point plan for a European technological community. The charges in Mr Benn's letter were calculated to appeal to strong Common Market feeling against technological domination by America.

The letter can also be regarded as an unusual piece of British salesmanship to the Common Market. It refers specifically to the value of Britain's fast reactor technology to the whole of Europe.

By revealing officially for the first time that Westinghouse had tried to acquire a licence for British fast reactor know-how, the Minister proved that the American company was interested more in specific information than in making good their shortage in manpower.

Background for Interest

The deskman should write in background mainly for intelligibility but also for interest. A few extra words of detail add bite to a story. Rather than letting copy pass with a reference to 'Sharpeville', or worse, 'events at Sharpeville', the deskman writes in 'the Sharpeville riots when South African police shot and killed 67, and wounded 182'.

When a member of a legislature resigns, his winning margin of votes at the last election should be written in so that the political fortunes of his seat can be assessed. If there is a bad plane or train crash, the previous worst, and any similarities should be recalled. Sometimes the deskman with a good library can create a whole story by relating information already known to a new development—for instance, the agency flash which brought the news in 1961 that Russia had decided to resume testing nuclear weapons and would test a series of giant nuclear bombs with a claimed yield equivalent to 20, 30, 50 and 100 million tons of TNT.

Here the lines of development include the background on disarmament talks, and the interpretation of one hundred million tons of TNT into proportions the reader can grasp. The deskman sends for sets of clippings and can build up a story on the bald announcement. First the diplomatic side:

This ends the three-year-old truce on the testing of hydrogen bombs. The last known Soviet nuclear tests occurred on November 1 and November 3, 1958, within days of the start on October 31 of that year of the nuclear test-ban conference in Geneva.

The last United States test took place during October, 1958. The US declared that it would continue its suspension of nuclear testing on a voluntary basis, 'provided that no further tests were conducted after those in the early days of November, 1958.

The test-ban talks between Britain, the United States and Russia have been deadlocked for the past five months. During the talks the only known nuclear tester has been France.

The deskman could build the scientific background into a separate story.

The 100-megaton (100-million-ton) bomb, if it is ever tested, would cause barely imaginable devastation. The bomb the Americans dropped on Hiroshima in 1945 was equal to only 20,000 tons (20 kilotons) of TNT—and it wiped out 80,000 people in one explosion. The 100-megaton bomb is 5,000 times as powerful. Even the smaller of the bombs announced, the 20-megaton, can cause third-degree burns 45 miles away.

It is not long since bombs were weighed in pounds. When the last war began a 1,000lb bomb was enough to create terror among a civilian population. Four years later came the 'block-buster', which was *ten tons* of TNT, and then in March 1945 the Royal Air Force's 22-ton Grand Slam, the heaviest conventional bomb ever used operationally.

If the Russians go ahead with their tests they are bound to throw up radioactive debris which will drift over the world creating new fears of pollution.

As it happens, the biggest bomb tested was probably one of 57 megatons in the USSR on October 30, 1961—according to the *Guinness*

Book of Records, which is one of the easy sources for deskmen when a bare agency message needs fleshing out in a hurry.

The chance for this kind of creative editing comes more often than you may think: a recurrence of floods (check and write in what action was promised last time); a runaway lorry on a hill (check previous accidents and protests); a take-over bid (check all the ramifications). Perhaps the most familiar opportunity is the death of a well-known person. On a busy evening paper, especially, there will not be time to invite an accomplished obituary. The deskman will call at once for the library clippings and add as much as he can in the time available. It is usually best for the deskman to do this, rather than pass the task to a reporter, because the deskman can more easily weave into his story any further new agency information, such as tributes, the circumstances of death, or a note on political implications, and so on. Check the library clippings with *Who's Who*, if you can.

Another opportunity is the compendium story—when a series of similar events are pulled into one story. In an icy weekend there were five separate drownings on frozen ponds in different places. It was good copy-tasting and editing to pull them together into one story with a common intro:

> Five boys were drowned in accidents on frozen ponds over the weekend.

That is the general intro. If one incident is outstanding it can be made the intro, with a second general paragraph bringing in the other items.

At all times translate foreign figures into domestic—dollars into pounds (or vice versa), metres into yards; and give both. Relate everything to the ordinary life of the reader. Tell him what a 'pasteurised' egg is as well as a fast-breeder reactor; don't leave him guessing what an invisible export is—or where he could find Aldabra. Tell him where in the political spectrum is the French Radical Party. If you have to hesitate yourself before you write in the explanation, consider how much easier you are making things for the reader. Never let anything pass which you yourself would not be able to explain without the help of the library.

Story-telling

The discussion so far has been on straight news stories of two types: action and statement—opinion stories. The opening advocated in both is the same, to reveal at once the most dramatic or important human results of the activity. I would make one exception—the occasion when the news point is deliberately delayed for a sentence. That delay can add pith and contrast. It offers variety. And the news point is still high up in the story.

Delaying the point by a sentence or two is still essentially hard news treatment of a story. Delaying it beyond that—perhaps to the end of the report—is a technique, not of news reporting, but of story-telling. The technique is common in feature writing: 'How I escaped from the dreaded Wonga tribesmen', says the headline and the writer begins with the day he caught the boat train. The story begins at the beginning and goes step by step to its stirring conclusion. The emphasis of the story is not what happened but how it happened. The technique is clearly distinct from the hard news treatment of an action story.

For most hard news stories story-telling is too slow a technique. It is exasperating to the reader who wants to find out what happened. But story-telling has its uses even in news columns. There is a certain monotony when every story on every page opens with the same hard news urgency. Story-telling provides a change of pace. It is most useful of all in popular newspapers which package news as entertainment, and for weekly news magazines and newspapers who are behind the dailies with the hard news, but who have extra detail to relate. But story-telling must be used frugally. It must never be the most prevalent structure.

Let us look at the two forms of treatment. First the straight news report. It meets all our tests of being direct, active and human:

> Several American marines were hurt yesterday when they walked into a minefield outside their camp.
>
> They were following a 14-year-old Vietnamese boy who later admitted that he had laid the minefield himself. He said he had been tortured by the Vietcong to do it.
>
> The Marines said he was a 'cute little guy' who hung around the camp gate asking questions. They had talked to him and answered his questions—on explosives.

The *Daily Mirror* treated this as an exercise in story-telling:

> American Marines at a camp in Vietnam thought that the friendly

14-year-old Vietnamese boy was a 'cute little guy'.

He would hang around the camp gates asking questions.

The Marines told him what he wanted to know . . . about explosives.

Then one day the boy led a number of the Marines into a minefield outside the camp—a minefield he had laid himself.

, Some of the Marines were hurt.

The boy, caught later, said he had been tortured by the Communist Vietcong into doing it.

The first version would have been quite acceptable to many newspapers. But anyone editing on any paper which tries to make a popular appeal you will often be impelled to use the story-telling technique.

The following story has the customary hard news intro—when the hard news is really not there to justify the report's position as a news story:

Margate Corporation will today receive a rear-door flap for a dust cart—which had been 21 days on its way by railway.

British Rail said: 'With a continued heavy flow of traffic it. is regretted that the consignment in question, having been off-loaded into Platform 2, has not yet been sent on its way, but it will be delivered tomorrow.'

Passengers on the 5.41 p.m. from King's Cross to Welwyn Garden City were puzzled by the large crate addressed to Margate Corporation standing on a platform for more than a fortnight. So one of them wrote to the Town Clerk, Margate, and the Stationmaster at King's Cross.

The only element of interest in this story is that curious passengers saved Margate's rear-door flap. The story could be given a livelier beginning in the hard news style:

Commuters on the 5.41 p.m. King's Cross to Welwyn Garden City helped to equip a Margate Corporation dust cart yesterday.

Puzzled by the large crate for Margate standing untouched on their platform 2 for more than a fortnight they wrote to Margate Corporation and King's Cross stationmaster.

The crate contained . . .

The *Evening Standard* made the most of the news item by adopting the story-telling technique:

The enormous, gunmetal-grey crate on Platform 2 at King's Cross, addressed to Margate Corporation, intrigued the commuters on the 5.41 p.m. to Welwyn Garden City. Every night they examined it and wondered what could be inside.

Until today . . . more than a fortnight later . . . they could stand the suspense no longer.

And their spokesman, solicitor Mr. W. J. Shaw, wrote to the Town Clerk at Margate and the Stationmaster at King's Cross.

'It seems amazing that British Rail can leave consignments, which may be urgent, lying around on a station for weeks,' said Mr. Shaw at his Holborn office this afternoon.

What IS in the 6ft × 4ft crate which weighs 1cwt 56lb?

A rear-door flap for one of Margate's dust carts.

It was despatched from the Letchworth engineering firm of Shelvoke and Drewery on August 27.

Said a spokesman for British Rail: 'With a continued heavy flow of traffic it is regretted that the consignment in question, having been off-loaded into Platform 2, has not yet been sent on its way.'

This afternoon the dust-cart flap is on its way to Margate and should arrive tomorrow.

It will have taken 21 days.

The story-telling structure is ideal for routine court reports. The court reports in some serious newspapers may be published for the significance of the legal judgment, and, in local papers, for the familiar names of those involved. For very many newspapers, however, it is neither of these news points which attracts. The court reports are published for the human drama they provide. Names and legal sequels are the small print in the credits column of a theatrical programme. Of course, the deskman must take great care to tell only the story supported by the judgment and by what the witnesses said in court. If there is a doubt it should be resolved in favour of the straightforward report. It is better to bore a thousand readers than to defame one.

Here is a straightforward court report:

> Four factory workers were fined a total of £14 for using intimidating behaviour against a fellow worker at West Bromwich magistrates court yesterday.
>
> They were.... They were accused of intimidating 32-year-old Lester Seville, a tool setter of Blackthorne Road, Walsall, who had not joined a strike, now 13 weeks old, at the factory, Newmans Tubes Ltd, Wednesbury.
>
> Charges of using threatening behaviour were dismissed.
>
> Mr Seville told the court the four men were pickets who stopped him one night when he left the factory to try and persuade him to join the strike. 'I was frightened because of their attitude', he said. They were quite prepared to use 'a little bit of pressure.'
>
> Mr George Jones, defending, said the men merely wanted to hold a quiet conversation with Seville.

Using the story-telling technique, the deskman would select the point where the action began and build the story from there.

> Four pickets lay in wait one night for a fellow worker—to try to persuade him to join a strike.
>
> And they were quite prepared to use 'a little bit of pressure', according to the worker, 32-year-old Lester Seville.
>
> 'I was frightened because of their attitude,' he told magistrates at

West Bromwich, Staffordshire, yesterday.

It happened during a strike, now 13 weeks old, at Newmans Tubes Ltd, Wednesbury.

Mr George Jones, defending four men before the court, said that they merely wanted to hold a quiet conversation with Mr Seville, a tool setter, of Blackthorne Road, Walsall.

At no time did they use any force or threats.

The four accused . . . were fined a total of £14 for using intimidating behaviour.

Charges of using threatening behaviour were dismissed.

The source of news reports may be delayed even more. It is not until the sixth paragraph here that the reader is told this is a court report. (The headline: 'Golfer takes a swing at the Sergeant'). Paragraph 6 is worth your attention. It is the link between the yarn and its source.

Golfer Sidney McCallum lost his temper, took a swing . . . and broke a policeman's jaw.

It happened between the eight and ninth holes on the Richmond Park golf course, Surrey.

McCallum, a 42-year-old cable jointer, of Petersfield Rise, Putney, London SW—'a fairly quick golfer' —was playing the course behind Sergeant Francis Bott.

And McCallum told the sergeant: 'Get a move on, you're slowing us up'.

Sgt Bott said: 'We can't go any quicker because of those chaps in front.'

Then, Mr K Hargreave, prosecuting, told the South Western magistrates court yesterday, the sergeant received 'a very hard blow.'

He was taken to hospital with a broken jaw, concussion and amnesia. He has lost six weeks' work but is expected to return on December 1.

McCallum later told police that Sgt. Bott had tried to throw him: 'I was out for a game of golf not a punch-up. I stepped back and hit him once.'

The magistrate, Sir John Cameron, told McCallum: 'Fortunately violence on the golf course is not very prevalent. I am not going to take as serious a view as if this had occurred on a football ground.'

He conditionally discharged McCallum for a year for causing bodily harm, but ordered him to pay £10 costs.

And so, too, with the reporting of wills. If one is working on a local paper, the news will be how much has been left and to whom. There is no substitute for the details here, presented directly as 'Mr X left . . . and his bequests were . . .' If the person involved is not well known or the sum not large, the popular national or big evening paper will generally expect the story edited so that the point is near the end rather than the beginning. They will not want:

Mrs Wells of Barton-on-Sea left a bottle of sherry and a bottle of gin in her will, announced yesterday, to a Gas Board official because he was cheerful when installing her central heating.

The executives will ask for a rewrite which makes the news into a tale:

Every time the man from the Gas Board called at Mrs Amy Wells's home, she changed her mind about the radiators she was having installed.

But the gasman kept on smiling.

And though he did not know it then, his smile had won him a friend.

Mr Lawrence Price, district sales manager of the Southern Gas Board, who supervised the installation of the radiators two years ago, heard last night that Mrs Wells, of Barton-on-Sea, Hampshire, had remembered him in her £11,655 will.

Mrs Wells, who was 82 when she died, left him a bottle of gin and a bottle of sherry—'for keeping on smiling every time I changed my mind.'

News-features Editing

These last snippets are really in the no-man's land between news and features, the writer making the most of flimsy material. But the story-telling technique is not simply a gimmick the deskman should learn for popular papers. Here is a serious example from a *New York Times* feature where the delayed intro is well used to contrast the start and the pinnacle of a man's career.

> When he was growing up in Stoughton, Wis., during the early 1920s, H. I. Romnes used to think of himself as a 'lucky fellow'. As the oldest of five children, Mr. Romnes was what he calls the 'front man' and did the selling in his father's bakery shop while the others stoked the fires and kneaded the dough.
>
> Last week, after two years as president, Mr. Romnes once again became the man up front when he was named chairman and chief executive officer of the American Telephone and Telegraph Company.

News magazines and serious weekly newspapers have to use delayed intros and story-telling techniques to do justice to assessments and complicated investigative reports. If the subject has not been running in the news but comes from the paper's own inquiries, it may be essential for the writer to put his conclusions into context. In this *Sunday Times* Insight article in 1966 the delayed intro does that—and it effectively contrasts promise in 1964 and performance in 1966:

> In July, 1964, Peter Thorneycroft, then Minister of Defence, rose to answer an awkward Parliamentary question about the size of the Ministry's senior staff. 'I have been able to take certain actions,' he told Labour MP James Boyden, 'which ensure that Professor Parkinson is removed from the establishment.'
>
> Three months earlier Thorneycroft had proudly introduced his 'revolutionary' streamlined Ministry, designed to impose greater central control on defence policy. Two and a half years after the revolution, an Insight inquiry has found

that the Ministry, under Thorney-croft's successor, Denis Healey, is not the streamlined instrument it should be. Parkinsonism, far from being uprooted, is spreading.

Instead of fewer senior officials, there are more. Instead of a controlled system of decision-making on a tri-service basis, decisions are made tortuously by an elaborate and inefficient committee system. Instead of the services cutting their inflated strengths, they cling stubbornly to an archaic career structure.

This article is neither straight news nor feature; it is a mixture of news and opinion. A straight news intro would have said 'There are more officials in the Ministry of Defence instead of fewer promised by Mr Peter Thorneycroft in July, 1964'. That would have been all right as far as it went, but it would have been thin and flat by comparison with the story-telling style. The writer properly preferred to use the jaunty scene in Parliament two years earlier as an overture for the repetitive discordant notes in the third paragraph. The three separate sentences there, as well as adding emphasis by the use of 'instead of . . .' also come to grips with a rather more complicated set of conclusions than could comfortably be housed in a straight news sentence.

This third paragraph is what is often called a 'taster'—a taste for the reader of things to come. It is a kind of trailer, a come-on to the reader confronted with a lot of words. Where you are editing a very long feature report, say 2,000 words or more, you should see that the structure accommodates early appetisers of some of the good things developed later in the narrative:

At 9.30 a.m. on his last day in England, May 25, 1951, Donald Maclean was walking decorously from Charing Cross station to his room in the Foreign Office. Guy Burgess, never a devotee of early rising, had only just got out of bed in his New Bond Street flat by Aspreys. He was reading *The Times* and drinking tea made by his friend Jack Hewit. Everything was relaxed and unhurried.

By 10.30 everything had changed, irrevocably. Burgess, warned

Opening with a dramatic human highlight. It is out of sequence in the article but essential to capture interest.

through Kim Philby in Washington that Donald Maclean was about to be interrogated, made a vital decision. By that evening Maclean had gone, in a cloud of mystery—and Burgess had gone with him.

But for Burgess's excited and unnecessary flight, things might have been very different for Kim Philby. Conceivably, the most remarkable Soviet spy ever to penetrate the Western intelligence community might have remained undetected for another ten years. Certainly it is now clear that it was only his almost fortuitous double link—with both Burgess and Maclean—which turned suspicion on him.

Had the cool, untrusting Philby been finally betrayed in 1951 by the bonds of Burgess's impulsive friendship, it would have been an ironic finale. But the damage Burgess did to him was more than compensated by the inflexible loyalty of his friends in the Secret Intelligence Service. Insight's inquiries have now established in detail that Philby, publicly sacked from the Foreign Service in 1951, was in fact secretly employed as a British agent by the SIS—even during the shadowy period before he became an *Observer* foreign correspondent at the request of the Foreign Office.

Feelings about Kim Philby vary sharply among his old colleagues in the British Secret Intelligence Service. Some preserve a degree of affection, and ruminate upon the 'misplaced idealism' which led him to work for the Russians. Some see his career largely as a technical feat. 'He was an agent who really lived his cover', they say.

Others take a more impassioned view, like the man who said to us: 'Philby was a copper-bottomed bastard, and he killed a lot of people.'

Espionage and counter-espionage can seem so much like civilised office-games that the blood can get forgotten. But in this account of

Recapitulation. Early presentation of an important conclusion.

Philby's career from 1945 to 1951 there are two crucial episodes which luridly illuminate the realities of the game.

The first case is a man alone: a Soviet intelligence officer caught in the act of trying to defect to the West. That story ends with a bandaged figure being hustled aboard a Russian plane in Istanbul.

Taster No. 1. Will be told in detail later.

In the second case, there are some 300 men in armed parties, slipping across the Iron Curtain border from Greece into Albania. This was a scheme designed to test the feasibility of breaking Communist control of Eastern Europe by subversion: the story ends in a crackle of small-arms fire on bleak hillsides, and the total discrediting of a policy which might have caused the Soviet Government a lot of trouble.

Taster No. 2. Will be told in detail later.

Behind each case is the shadow of Kim Philby—the Soviet penetration-agent at the heart of the Secret Intelligence Service, the man whose loyalty went unquestioned for so long. Indeed, it might never have been questioned, but for the fact that Philby was caught up in the complex aftermath of Donald Maclean's espionage for the Russians.

Recapitulation, to remind readers of the essence of the story. New development indicated.

Most good news and feature leads have one thing in common: they are specific and human. Indeed, the way the news magazine or weekly copes with beginning a story that has been running in the daily papers is to be more specific and detailed about some element in it. The news stories had already said, for instance, that King Constantine of Greece had tried to overthrow the military government and had flown to Rome after his failure. A later news-feature treatment of that story could have begun *at any point where the writer had sufficient vivid detail*, preferably new, to arouse the reader's interest. The news report has to be built on the latest information. The news-feature report begins on the most vivid sequence in the whole chronology of the story. *Time* magazine began its report of the King's revolt like this:

To the astonishment of a handful of passengers waiting at Rome's Ciampino Airport at 4 a.m. squads of

Italian police suddenly materialized and took up positions around the field. Moments later, a white turbo-prop jet taxied to a stop on the apron. In the plane's doorway appeared a young man in the red-trimmed uniform of a field marshal. Limping slightly from fatigue, his face ashen and heavily bearded, King Constantine of Greece, 27, walked down a ramp on to Italian soil. Behind him, glum and red-eyed, came his Danish wife, Queen Anne-Marie, 25, her mink coat still smelling of the mothballs from which she had hastily removed it.

With them were their two infant children, Queen Mother Frederika, the King's 25-year-old sister Irene, and several loyal followers.

Thus last week, after an abortive royal countercoup that may go down as one of the most inept conspiracies in history, the King of the Hellenes fled his country, leaving in control more firmly than ever the military junta that had seized power last April in a lightning coup.

Where the news result is familiar to readers, detail is the only answer. *The Sunday Times* reconstruction of the Rhodesian talks between Harold Wilson and Ian Smith on board HMS Tiger began like this, with new detail of a dramatic moment in the talks:

The first intimation that the Tiger talks might be a flop came just three hours before the end of the seaborne confrontation. Mr Ian Smith, the Rhodesian Premier, was showing extreme reluctance to put his signature to the working document that he had personally elaborated with the British negotiators in the previous day. 'If you won't sign,' said Mr Wilson, settling for half a loaf, 'you will of course commend it to your Government colleagues in Salisbury.' 'I'll have to commend it to myself first, won't I?', said Smith.

Detail, not chronology, must be the master in feature leads. The detail can even be a development since the hard news was first told. This was the beginning of a feature telling how commercial television companies had competed for new franchises in Britain:

> Every morning on a private line between the commercial television companies there is a grandly-styled Red Telephone Conversation: the network planning officers of the 14 companies use it to synchronise their complicated programme swaps. Last Thursday the exchanges were somewhat chilled.
>
> Rediffusion, in the chair, was attempting to explain how the night before it had managed to help perpetrate one of the network's biggest programme muddles. Bewildered viewers outside London had been treated to a discussion of the documentary 'Famine', which they were told they had just seen—but which, in fact, had gone out only to London viewers.
>
> The 'Famine' mix-up seems to have been the first unlooked-for product of last Sunday's announcement by the Independent Television Authority of the new franchise deal for 1968—bringing three new companies into the business; deposing Television West and Wales and cutting Rediffusion's programme days effectively from five days to two. Rediffusion just has not been the same since.

The features editor should study the structure of the best feature stories in the newspapers and news magazines. Features deskmen are not there to write features: that is the job of the writers. But the features man should be able to tell a writer what is wrong with the structure of a story; he should be able to make suggestions for improvement. I say 'suggestions' because there should be time in features editing to discuss improvements with the writer. Features deskmen can make real improvements in both the language and structure of pieces presented even by brilliant writers: occasionally the specialist overlooks the ignorance of the average reader; new features writers are often on an adjectival spree or simply out to show their skill.

The features editor should always put his observations to even the best writers—but where there is a margin of doubt he should always give the writer the preference and he should not hack good writing to preconceived notions. If you have gone to features editing from straight news editing, beware the reflex actions you have rightly cultivated as a straight-news man. In features, the mood, the style may be everything. This is also true of the news-features which can appear on a news page, the occasions when a descriptive commentator is covering a news scene and there is no hard news at that precise moment. For instance, here is a news-feature intro from Aden by David Holden:

> 'Gone away' says the sign painted on the wall of Aden's biggest prison by some waggish British soldier a couple of months ago when the last of South Arabia's political detainees were released. 'Gone away—no milk, no papers.'
>
> The sign is still there; and in two or three weeks from now when the last British troops leave Aden for good, it may well serve as a mocking epitaph for 128 years of empire in South Arabia.
>
> In Aden, the empire was never very imperial and, apart from 'Ali Baba's' mobile chip shop, it is not leaving much behind. Already this is a half-abandoned city.

A sub with an itching pencil might have been tempted to rewrite a hard news intro: 'Already Aden is a half-abandoned city'. That would, of course have ruined an evocative intro which had woven into it some of the background and a news point which was much more tellingly made in the context. Gone away, gone away . . . the desolation is vivid.

As a final caution, read this intro. The hard news was simply that Irish people were being asked to stay in England for Christmas because of the risk of spreading foot-and-mouth disease. Peter Dunn had visited some of the Irish stranded for Christmas, and he might easily have begun: 'Christmas dinner has been specially laid on for some 250 Irishmen stranded in London by the foot-and-mouth restrictions.'

Instead he chose a detail—a specific human Irish detail which makes us want to delve deeper:

> Mr. Allen C. Breeze, Irish poet,
> author of Tshombe's Lament and
> owner of T. S. Eliot's false teeth,
> will not be going home to Ireland
> this Christmas, though he had
> planned to. He has given his air
> ticket to his friend, Charlie, a tall
> serious man who is in commerce.

Intros like this still the itchiest subbing fingers.

8 Accuracy and House Style

A sub-editor, though possessed of more than the ordinary share of infallibility, sometimes gets the wrong sow by the ear. —F. J. MANSFIELD

Much of the ground in text editing has now been covered. It remains to summarise and emphasise a few general points, under the headings of accuracy, the law, newspaper style and reference books.

Accuracy

At every stage in communication there is a risk of distortion and error. The deskman has to reverse this natural tendency. He will, being fallible, introduce error, but for every one he perpetrates he should have a moral bank balance of a thousand errors apprehended. The traps lie in rewriting and alteration on copy. When copy is rewritten it should always, at the end, be checked with the original. Every name, title, date and figure should be compared letter by letter, digit by digit. Who said what in the original should be checked with who says what in edited copy.

It is easy to misattribute quotes. Headline words should be checked with copy, too. In front of me is a 72-pt headline for the front-page lead in a national daily saying: 'US lends £400m to Britain'. The copy says the £400m 'stand-by credit' is from the International Monetary Fund. As for the reporter's original copy, too, the deskman must cultivate a nasty scepticism. Is this man really the chairman of this company, as the copy says, or is his title managing director? Can you really build a public swimming baths for £13,000? Is Ghana really 'next door' to Nigeria? Every fact without a halo should be checked in the reference books and library clippings (see below). Who did what, when and where? Sentences must be fingered for hidden meanings; commas should never be trusted. It is better to say, 'The judge said Smith was an evil man', than 'Smith, said the judge, was an evil man'. Commas are easily missed out by the printer and often never print clearly, anyway. Particular care must be taken with foreign names, court copy, and telephone copy

where mishearings and mistypings can slip through into the collectors'
books:

The Boston forwards were too fat for the defence (fast)

Ivor Novello's musical play Careless Rupture (Rapture)

A woman of humble girth (birth)

B . . . who is on the black market (B. is a golf backmarker)

'The trouble with young blaggards like you' (blackguards)

The bazaar was opened by the county surveyor (Countess of Ayr)

Dr. . . . gave a talk on 'Youth in Asia' (euthanasia)

Antonia Evanescent, the well-known Communist . . . (economist)

Figures are another trap. Add up the percentages to see that they
reach 100. Watch for transpositions which can easily occur in typing:
1699 or 1969? Where decimal points occur it is advisable to mark the
copy 1 dec 75 million, 23 dec 9 billion. A misplaced decimal point or
comma, particularly in money, may spell ruin for an investor-reader—
and the newspaper.

The Law

Legal pitfalls are touched on in the narrative of this series of books
where appropriate but every deskman should make a point of studying
books on newspaper law. This section discusses general points on libel,
contempt, and court reporting. It is based on English law, which is as
rigorous as anywhere in the world on libel and contempt, and illuminates
the constraints. But I have noted some important differences in the
United States and two good US reference books are included in the
bibliography.

Libel The classic definition is that an actionable defamatory libel is a
statement in some permanent form, published about a person whom it
exposes to hatred, ridicule or contempt or causes to be shunned or
avoided, or tends to injure in his office, profession or trade. A good
practical test is to substitute your own name for the one in the story and
ask: Would I like these facts about myself published? If the answer is
No, the copy is probably defamatory—but that does not mean the copy
should be spiked. Public affairs cannot be conducted without defama-

tion. Reputations are daily attacked in the courts, in legislatures and town halls, and reported, and newspapers themselves have a duty to expose wrong-doing.

But defamation is not libel. It is only libel when a court decides that the newspaper has failed to establish any one of three principal defences: these are (1) Justification, (2) Fair comment, (3) Privilege.

Justification means truth. If the paper can prove what it published to be true, it is the most complete and final defence to libel. Occasionally, even among journalists, the absurd maxim survives: 'the greater the truth, the greater the libel'. On the contrary. Anything can be published without fear which can be shown to be true. No public interest has to be demonstrated. The truth is considered sufficiently a public interest. Of course, proof is the thing. 'Knowing' something is true is not the same as proving it—and it rests with the newspaper to do the proving, not the injured party. The deskman about to publish a defamatory statement should see that the scope of proof that may be required is as narrow as possible.

Again, contrary to what many journalists seem to suppose, in defamation the specific allegation is less dangerous than the general allusion. In other words, to suggest that 'some councillors on the Fliphampton Council are obviously corrupt' is intrinsically much more dangerous than saying 'Councillors Smith and Jones of the Fliphampton Council are corrupt'. In the first example, there is likely to be an innuendo that damages entirely innocent members of the council—and it is a statement that can be held to defame anyone on the council. In the second example, there is a plain allegation which we can either stand up or not stand up—and we can only be sued by the people we name. In other words, smears are dangerous.

The principle that the specific allegation is intrinsically safer, and better journalism, is worth bearing in mind whenever considering stories which are likely to cause offence. For instance, it is safer (and usually better, as a piece of reporting) to say 'Olga Diva sang incompetently last night' than to say 'Olga Diva is an incompetent singer'.

The legal definition of hearsay evidence is complex, but the principle works like this. Wilson tells you that he saw Smith fighting in the street on New Year's Eve. Wilson can then, if it is necessary, give evidence in court about what he saw—or for that matter heard—on that occasion.

But a reporter cannot give evidence about what Wilson said to him about what Smith did. It does not matter how many people heard Wilson say it: it does not matter how true the allegation may be. Only

Wilson can give evidence about what he heard and saw. There are exceptions to the rule excluding hearsay evidence, but it is safe to count on them not applying.

The second defence to libel is that the defamation was 'fair comment on a matter of public interest'. The law gives wide latitude to strong opinions provided they are made in good faith and without malice. The newspaper will lose the defence of fair comment if it can be shown that it was moved by spite or twisted the facts on which to base its criticism. Malice is more easily shown if the attacks are persistent, so whenever an article of hostile comment is before you for editing, it is worth checking earlier references. The previous defence of justification, it should be added, survives proof of malice.

The third defence is privilege. There is absolute privilege for fair and accurate reports of English judicial proceedings, when such reports are published contemporaneously in a newspaper. However untrue, however malicious, a report made on an absolutely privileged occasion carries no risk. All that is required is that it be a fair and accurate report of proceedings heard in public, published contemporaneously with the proceedings and not containing any blasphemous or indecent material. What a newspaper has to watch is first that it does not give undue prominence to the prosecution case. If one side of a case is given in one edition or issue, the other must be added in later editions or issues. The newspaper, taken as a whole, must give a fair picture of the proceedings taken as a whole, as far as they have progressed by the time of publication.

Secondly, the newspaper must remember that the privilege is not simply for judicial matters but for public proceedings. Some court proceedings are private. There is no privilege for them if they are reported; there may indeed be the error of contempt. In Britain the commonest snare is proceedings in chambers. In the United States it would be contempt to report evidence before a grand jury because the proceedings are private. But it is safe to report the indictment (or absence of one) which results from the proceedings.

Similarly, it is safe to report a legal arrest, but there is no privilege for statements about the arrest from police or lawyers. In England and Scotland, they are probably contempt of court: in the US they must, if defamatory, be defended without the protection of privilege.

Finally, there is a qualified privilege. Here the report loses its privilege if it is shown to have been made maliciously or in bad faith. There are four main occasions of qualified privilege:

● A report of judicial proceedings, not published contemporaneously. The report must be fair and accurate. It must not be blasphemous or indecent and it must not have been prohibited by court order or statutory provisions.

● Reports of Parliamentary proceedings (debates and questions in the Commons and Lords, or of the proceedings of Congress), provided they are fair and accurate.

● Extracts from and abstracts of Parliamentary papers published by order or under the authority of the House of Commons or Lords; or of the US Congress; extracts from registers kept by order of statutes; and copies of documents open by law to public inspection. Wills and orders under the Bankruptcy Acts offer two instances. Again, the extract must be fair and accurate.

● A report of a lawful public meeting in the United Kingdom or of the meeting of a local authority provided it is (1) fair and accurate, (2) contains nothing blasphemous or indecent, and (3) is of public concern and for the public benefit. But note that some occasions of privilege, like these two instances, are conditional on publication of a reasonable letter or statement by way of explanation or contradiction.

These defences will seem to give a newspaper a good run, but a deskman publishing defamatory material must be convinced that one or more of the defences will apply. In both English and American law the defence of privilege fails if the newspaper publishes defamatory material extraneous to the privileged proceedings. Colourful descriptions of what happened in court, rather than straight reporting of evidence, are a trap. ('The witness looked distinctly uneasy when confronted with the document' may lead to the newspaper feeling distinctly uneasy when it is challenged for libel or contempt.) A follow-up to a story emanating from privileged or partially privileged proceedings must clearly stand on its own feet.

There are other fallacies. One is that a newspaper is safe if it is merely repeating what someone else alleged, perhaps in another newspaper or in a book. But it is not so. The injured person can sue whomever he likes. It is no defence to say the libel first appeared somewhere else. The newspaper, by publishing it, makes the libel its own and must take the responsibility.

It is another fallacy to think anything can be published about a bad character. A man with a damaged character is entitled to have his damaged character protected. Some journalists even think that it will do to tell the court that the libel was a slip: we didn't mean it. That, too, is no defence. What the writer meant the words to mean is irrelevant; it is what a jury can be persuaded to read into them that counts. Many a writer has been skinned by his own ingenious semantics.

American practice United States law follows English in many ways. But there are two important differences for the deskman—one helpful, one inhibiting.

The helpful one is the case of the *New York Times v. Sullivan* and its offspring, which the state courts there have been required to recognise. Sullivan was the Commissioner who supervised the Montgomery police department. He claimed he was defamed by an 'editorial advertisement' in the *New York Times*, placed there by a group of civil rights workers. Some of the statements in the advertisement were false—but in this classic case the defence did not thereby fail. The Supreme Court ruled that for critics of official conduct to have to guarantee the truth of all their factual statements would lead to 'self-censorship'. It would dampen the vigour and limit the variety of public debate—and that would be against the constitutional principle of free speech guaranteed by the First Amendment. The news media, the Court ruled, are not liable for defamatory words published in good faith about the public acts of public officials even if they cannot prove them to be substantially true. They are only in trouble if the public official can prove that the defamatory falsehood about him and his public work was made with 'actual malice'. And the court went on to define 'actual malice' in a vigorous way that has extended the protection of publishers. Malice thereafter has not to be proved by arguing 'ill will' or 'intent to harm' the defamed. To be guilty of malice, the publisher has now to publish a falsehood knowing it is a falsehood or in 'reckless disregard of the truth'.

What is 'reckless disregard'? And what is a 'public official'? These are two areas where the American deskman should prod the news department and consult the lawyers. In determining whether there is reckless diregard—which destroys the defence—the courts have taken into account whether the newspaper attempted to verify the defamatory statement before publishing and also the credibility of the source. The courts have ruled variously on whether the *New York Times* rule should be applied to people engaged in public controversy as much as to public officials.

PRIVACY LAW is a bugbear of American newspapers in most states which other countries have shown tendencies to copy. Damages can be awarded for statements which are true, which are free from defamation, and which are published with the best of intentions. A plaintiff can win by showing that the statements distressed or embarrassed his private life or put him in a 'false light'. Photographs and captions which might give a misleading impression of someone's character have proved especially dangerous: no deskman in the States should lightly re-use an old photograph of someone with a new caption to illustrate a general feature. If the person consents to the invasion of privacy, that is a good defence, and so is 'newsworthiness'; but the law of privacy, as one judge said, is like a haystack in a hurricane. There is a conflict from state to state and court jurisdiction to court jurisdiction, and deskmen have to watch the law's development.

Contempt of court   A deskman should refer to the editor any copy which lowers the authority of a court or which might prejudice a trial. In England and Scotland in particular the risks of a heavy fine or even a jail sentence for an editor are severe, and it is easy enough to publish by accident something which can be held to prejudice a trial.

The deskman should ask: Does this person or do these events figure in any way in court proceedings which are pending or imminent? If I were a potential juror would they in any way influence me? It does not matter which way the report leans, whether the information favours the defence or the prosecution. It does not matter whether the information is true. Evening paper deskmen must take particular care when a crime story is followed by news of an arrest. Any details on which there might be an argument in court must be cut from the original story.

It can also be dangerous to report a police statement about a man's previous record when bail is being decided: this would definitely be illegal in England under the Criminal Justice Act, 1967, unless the restrictions on publicity for committal proceedings had been lifted.

American courts have similar powers to English to cite newspaper editors for contempt where they publish pre-trial or during-trial material which might prejudice a defendant's right to a fair trial, but they have been very reluctant to use them. The Supreme Court has never upheld any such contempt conviction of any news medium (though it has ordered new trials for the defendants because of excessive pre-trial publicity). How far newspapers should use their freedom is a subject of some heat in the United States. The deskman seeking guidance should begin by studying the guidelines which were proposed

in 1965 by the former Attorney General, Nicholas de B. Katzenbach. [1]
Editing court copy Reporting of juvenile courts should not in any way identify the children. The word 'conviction' and 'sentence' must not be used. Reporting of matrimonial cases should not dwell on intimate detail. All that is permitted on this is a brief summary of the charges and counter-charges, and the judge's summing-up or final remarks.

Reports of magistrates' courts have been restricted in England since the Criminal Justice Act of 1967. Summary cases which the magistrates deal with can be reported freely, but where somebody faces an indictable charge (on which he may be sent for trial to a higher court) there are restrictions. If the charge is indictable all that may be reported is:

> The identity of the court and names of magistrates; names, addresses and ages of defendants and witnesses; the charges; names of counsel and solicitors; the decision of the court on committal or adjournment; arrangements about bail or legal aid.

Unrestricted reporting of committal cases is allowed (1) when one of the defendants facing indictment asks for publicity (the court has to agree to lift the ban); (2) when *all* are discharged; (3) when committal is for sentence only. Deskmen in Britain who receive an unrestricted report from a magistrates' court should see that one of the defendants is named in it as electing publicity or that all have been discharged. The idea is not to prejudice the later trial by reporting prosecution evidence.

Other points to watch in editing legal reports:

CHARGES: In all court cases the deskman must be sure what the charges are, and, if several people are charged, be sure that the copy makes it clear which charges apply to which people. That word 'charge' means a police allegation. It is safe to say X was charged with theft. It is emphatically not safe to say X was summoned for theft. 'Summons' does not have the qualification that it is an allegation. The report should say X appeared on a summons alleging theft, or X was summoned for alleged theft. We must never delete that an accused person 'elected' to go for trial; there is a big difference between this and being committed for trial.

EVIDENCE: If the copy says someone smiled or broke down in tears, it can be left in. But anything which implies comment must be cut:

---

[1] They are set out in *Law of Mass Communications* (*see* bibliography), p. 239, where there is an excellent discussion of the issues.

'Smith replied after hesitation'. There is no privilege for anything which is not part of the proceedings, e.g. an outburst from the public gallery of the court.

SENTENCE: Generally do not leave the verdict to the end. It may be unfair, and it could be dropped off on the stone. Never say in a General Medical Council Disciplinary Committee case that a doctor is to be struck off. Doctors have twenty-eight days to appeal. The phrase should be 'ordered to be struck off' and the right of appeal should be mentioned. Similarly, in reports of Army and RAF courts martial, it should always be added that the sentence is subject to confirmation. References to bail should always be kept in. Above all, deskmen must take tender care of the guilty or not guilty references. Agency copy deliberately repeats Not guilty (repeat NOT GUILTY). It is a safeguard staffmen should copy. The deskman deletes the parenthetical reminder but it remains visible to prudent editors. When the copy says 'guilty' check the rest of the story for consistency. Every 'guilty' story should have a penalty. Where there is a 'guilty' story without one, the 'not' may somewhere have been omitted.

BANKNOTES: It is an offence to publish a representation of a banknote or currency note—or even to have a block made.

SPORT: Never describe a competitor as 'veteran' unless he is in a contest officially described as veteran. Be careful with descriptions of any physical defect in any professional sportsman: and never let a boxing report say a boxer was disqualified for a low punch unless the referee has said that in an announcement. 'Disqualified after a body punch' will do.

Newspaper Style

The larger newspaper offices have 'style books' which may be a small book or merely a few sheets of a grubby quarto, that may be up to date or allowed to become obsolete. First-class style books are produced by the Chicago (Ill.) *Sun–Times*, the Boston *Globe*, the London *Times*, and the Toronto *Star*—and, of course, *The New York Times*, which has published its style book for public sale.[2] The style book alphabetically lists standardised spellings, typographical styles, banned words, dangerous

---

[2] *The New York Times Style Book for Editors and Writers*, edited and revised by Lewis Jordan (New York: McGraw Hill, 1962).

practices and rules for special subjects. Newspapers have different rules; the deskman must learn the rules of his own house. Behind some entries there is clearly a costly experience which the deskman will repeat at his peril (such as inaccurately identifying a branded product in a nasty inquest). But even small matters like whether Nato takes an initial cap are worth fussing about for two reasons. If the deskman lets through NATO all in caps, somebody else may be letting it through Nato. The printer may set it whichever way asked, and if it varies in style such erratic treatment is irritating to the reader. Secondly, if the deskman fails but the proof reader spots a variation from house style, a line of type or more has to be reset. This wastes time and money. There is no point in giving a complete style list here because of the variation from office to office. What I have done is present a few of the more important possible entries to give a deskman an idea of the ground a style verbal book should cover. The entry on trade names and titles, for instance, is universally valid.

Appellations Except for the Burmese, e.g. U Thant, refer to everyone as Mr, Mrs, etc., whatever their nationality. No full points after Mr, Mrs, Dr, Prof. Write service titles out in full on first mention; thereafter abbreviate. Mr is not used with names of sports people in sports pages but if they appear in the news section the Mr is used. Mr is not needed with names of famous people now dead.

Addresses Omit number but do not abbreviate street, road, etc. For non-London readers, London districts should be written thus: Piccadilly, London (Manchester also has a Piccadilly). Devon, Dorset, Somerset, Merioneth need no shire. Other English and Welsh county names are spelled out fully. Do not use Salop or Oxon. Scottish county names are not abbreviated except for the omission of shire. Beware of double-places: there are three Farnboroughs and fifteen Carltons. Always give the county or state.

Banned kiddies, Reds, mystery surrounds, the police are baffled, floral tributes, night attire, Britisher, alerted, pooch (for dog), biggest ever, the small screen (for TV), nationwide (in UK), secret wedding, gutted, top model, pinta.

Capital letters Avoid using them unnecessarily. The Parks Committee, but subsequently the committee; the South-West Regional Hospital Board, but then the hospital board; so-and-so was elected chairman (not Chairman) and the chairman said. Alderman T. Jones, but then the alderman said. Some words need capitals in the largest sense: the Bench (left a lucrative practice for the Bench, but local benches of magistrates), the Army (but his army boots), the Church (a battle of Church against State), but the church down the road, more state control.

Don't cap alsatian, pekinese (dogs), siamese, persian (cats), french polish, bingo, housey-housey or other non-patented games, spring, summer, autumn (fall), winter, transatlantic, the trade union movement, whites. Do cap Negro, Magna Carta, Spiritualism, Roman Catholic.

Collective nouns Treat as singular, e.g. the Government is, Rootes is, and even Sniffel Bros and Sons is. And the committee, council is.

Grammar Deskmen are assumed to have a working knowledge of English grammar. Here, as a reminder, is a set of un-rules provided by Helen Ferril, of the *Rocky Mountain News*:

1. Don't use no double negative.
2. Make each pronoun agree with their antecedent.
3. Join clauses good, like a conjunction should.
4. About them sentence fragments.
5. When dangling, watch your participles.
6. Verbs has to agree with their subjects.
7. Just between you and I, case is important too.
8. Don't write run-on sentences they are hard to read.
9. Don't use commas, which aren't necessary.
10. Try to not ever split infinitives.
11. It's important to use your apostrophe's correctly.
12. Proofread your writing to see if you any words out.
13. Correct spelling is esential.

Organisations Unless as well known as the BBC always write out in full at first mention. If abbreviation is all caps, e.g. US, omit full points between, use hairline space between letters. If abbreviation sounds like a word, e.g. Nato, cap first letter only.

Ships Never say that Lady X launched the ship. The woman who releases the champagne bottle *names* the ship and does not usually launch it. It is launched by the shipbuilders. Never call ships 'boats'. Use HMS, USS, etc., for naval vessels; do not use s.s. for ships owned by commercial lines.

Science Scientific units are internationally agreed and should be given correctly. Mistakes may alter meaning or make nonsense. Abbreviations especially need to be watched, not least when writing out units in full from a source in which they are abbreviated. Only in. (for 'inch') needs a full point.

Television TV—only in headlines where necessary (note no points); commercial, independent television (l.c.). Never say ITV—you possibly mean ITA, ITN, or one of the companies. Avoid newscaster; say viewer not televiewer.

Titles Peerages, etc.: use reference books—*Kelly's Handbook to the Titled, Landed and Official Classes*; *Debrett's Peerage*; *Burke's Peerage, Baronetage and Knightage*; *Dod's* and *Vacher's Parliamentary Companion*; *Who's Who*.

General rules: Dukes are always dukes. Marquesses, earls and viscounts take their full title first time and thereafter are Lord Blank. Barons are always called Lord Blank (unless it is a foreign title). Baronets and knights are Sir John Blank first time, thereafter Sir John. Similarly with the title Dame: Dame Edith Evans first, then Dame Edith.

Church titles Use reference books—*Crockford's Clerical Directory* (Church of England); *The Catholic Directory*; *The Jewish Year Book*; *Who's Who in the Free Churches*. Archbishops and Bishops: first time, the Archbishop (Bishop) of X, Dr John Blank; thereafter Dr Blank. Exceptions: Roman Catholic Cardinals, e.g. Cardinal Heenan, Archbishop of Westminster, first mention; thereafter Cardinal Heenan or the Cardinal. Also some RC archbishops and bishops are not doctors of divinity. In these cases first reference should be the Bishop of X, the Rt. Rev John Blank; thereafter Bishop Blank.

Reverend must always be followed by the christian name (or initial at least), e.g. Rev John Smith. After first reference Mr Smith, or for Roman Catholic priests—Father Smith.

Senator Do not abbreviate even in headlines.

Trade names Some 'household words' are trade names. They are proprietary and require an initial cap. Beware of misuses which may be actionable. Since their mention is a free advertisement it is better to avoid them whenever possible. Some alternatives are bracketed:

Autogiro (helicopter)
Aertex (cellular clothing)
Aspro (aspirin)
Breathalyser (breath test device)

Bakelite (plastic)
Biro (ballpoint pen)
Brilon
BriNylon
Calor Gas (gas)
Catseyes (road studs)
Cellophane (transparent)
Cinemascope (wide-screen film)
Crombie (overcoat)
Coke (soft drink)
Celanese (Rayon, artificial silk)
Coalite (smokeless fuel)
Dictaphone (dictating machine)
Dixie (paper or plastic cups, plates, etc.)
Elastoplast (plaster)
Electrolux (vacuum cleaner)
Fibreglass (glass fibre)
Formica (laminated plastic)
Hoover (vacuum cleaner)
Hovercraft
Jeep (field car, scout car)
Kleenex (tissues, towels, table napkins, toilet paper)
Liberty bodice (knitted bodice)
Linotype (typesetting machine)
Landrover (field car, scout car)
Meccano (building kit)
Nescafe (instant coffee)
Perspex
Photostat (photo-copy)
Plasticine (modelling clay)
Polaroid
Primus-stove (oil stove)
Pyrex (heat-resistant glassware)
Rediffusion (relay television/radio)
Sellotape (sticking tape)
Tarmac (macadam)
Technicolor (colour)
TelePrompTer (cuing apparatus)
Terylene
Teletype

Vaseline (petroleum jelly, hair tonic)
Wedgwood (porcelain, chinaware)
Xerox (dry duplicator)

Reference Books

The first book to have is *Facts and How to Find Them* by William A. Bagley (London: Pitman, 1965). This is a reference book to the reference books. It is essential for a deskman to know where he can find what and quickly. When there is a spare moment, take down the copy of *Whitaker's Almanack*, the supreme year book for Britain; or, in the US, *The World Almanac and Book of Facts*, or *Information Please (USA)*. Turn over the pages and see what you can discover. How many people were convicted for betting and gaming last year? How big is the Queen Elizabeth II? Who owns her? What is the pay of an army private? How many undergraduates are there at Oxford University? What did the tax on cigarettes yield last year? Which country's babies die youngest? Then turn to the index and see how the book guides you to this information and the rest. Knowing which books tell what is only part of a deskman's skill; it is knowing how to use the book in a hurry that counts. I remember the first time I tried to check a current affairs fact in *Keesing's Contemporary Archives*. It is an admirable and indispensable guide, but the edition of my paper carrying the story had come and gone before I mastered the indexing system. (The equivalent American publication is *Facts on File*.)

A common mistake in consulting encyclopedias is to go for the alphabetical volume because articles are arranged alphabetically. It can be another source of frustration. To find the detail you want may mean following dozens of cross-references from the first general article. Always begin with the index volume.

A newspaper's own library of clippings needs to be approached in the same way. To check a detail, it is no use asking for 'the packet' on the Duke of Edinburgh. Most of the prominent people in public life acquire subdivided personal files. The deskman must be specific and understand his own library's system: it is worth remembering, too, that the librarians will feel more kindly disposed to staffmen who return the clippings in good order. Newspaper clippings libraries sometimes store error which a deskman reproduces; check that the packet contains no errata slip, or cross-references which may hold an errata slip. Deskmen rely so much on clippings that they will gain by reading the librarians' textbook on press-cutting libraries, *News Information*, by Geoffrey Whatmore (London: Crosby Lockwood, 1964).

It is not for this book to summarise the information that can be found in all the reference books. William Bagley's book does that. But here is a short list of references which the deskman should get to know. Essential books are indicated by an asterisk. Telephone directories, and a reminder that the current electoral roll lists names (addresses also, but these need to be checked), can be added to the list. A reader may forgive you for misdating the Boston tea party. He will never forgive a mistake in his name or initials.

General references
*Encyclopaedia Britannica or Chambers Encyclopedia
*Whitaker's Almanack
*Guinness Book of Records
*Pears Cyclopaedia
*Jane's Fighting Ships and Jane's All the World's Aircraft

Dictionaries
*Oxford English Dictionary: The Shorter Oxford in two volumes
*H. W. Fowler's Modern English Usage
  Usage and Abusage, by Eric Partridge
*Roget's Thesaurus of English Words and Phrases
  Black's Medical Dictionary
  World List of Abbreviations
  Pitman's Book of Synonyms & Antonyms

People
*Who's Who
  Who's Who in America
  Who's Who in Canada
  World Biography
*International Who's Who
  Dictionary of National Biography
*Kelly's Handbook to the Titled, Landed and Official Classes
  Burke's Peerage, Baronetage and Knightage
  Debrett's Peerage
  Medical Register and Medical Directory
  Law List
  Politics & Current Affairs

Vacher's Parliamentary Companion (quarterly)
*Dod's Parliamentary Companion (annually)
International Year Book and Statesman's Who's Who
The United States in World Affairs
*Keesing's Contemporary Archives
Facts on File
The Times Guide to the House of Commons
Army List
Civil Service List
Navy List
Foreign Office List
Air Force List
Colonial Office List
Britain (COI Handbook)
*Municipal Year Book

Places
Kelly's Directories for counties, cities and towns
*Bartholomew's Survey Gazetteer of the British Isles
*Times Atlas and World Gazetteer
AA and RAC Handbooks

Industry and commerce
Who Owns Whom
Kelly's Directory of Merchants, Manufacturers and Shippers
Directory of Employers' Associations, Trade Unions and Joint
  Organisations.
*Stock Exchange Year Books
Lloyd's Register of Shipping and Lloyd's Register of Yachts
Local Chamber of Commerce Directory
Directory of Directors

Historical
Dictionary of National Biography
Who Was Who
Haydn's Dictionary of Dates and Universal Information

Churches
*Crockford's Clerical Directory
The Catholic Directory

Who's Who in the Free Churches
The Jewish Year Book

Press, Theatre, TV
Who's Who in the Theatre
Who's Who in Show Business
Authors' and Writers' Who's Who
A Dictionary of Art and Artists
BBC Handbook
Who's Who in Music
TV and Radio Who's Who
International Television Almanac
International Motion Picture Almanac
Newspaper Press Directory
Editor and Publisher Year Book (USA)
Willing's Press Guide
Writer's and Artist's Year Book
Authors' and Printers' Dictionary

Science
Applied Science and Technology Index (USA)
Index to Current Technical Literature (USA)
Association of Special Libraries and Information Bureaux
    Directory

Sport
Football Association Year Book
Playfair's Football Annual
Wisden's Cricketer's Annual
Playfair's Cricket Annual
Playfair's Rugby Annual

9 Editing Exercises

If you want a thought that's happy
            Boil it down
Make it short and crisp and snappy
            Boil it down
When your brain its coin has minted
Down the page your pen has sprinted
If you want your effort printed
            Boil it down
Cut out all the extra trimmings
            Boil it down
Skim it well, then skim the skimmings
            Boil it down
When you're sure 'twould be a sin to
Cut another sentence into
Send it on and we'll begin to
            Boil it down

—THE WRITER'S LITANY

This chapter is composed of newspaper reports. All were published in British or American newspapers. All have had some kind of editorial scrutiny. Yet they exhibit many of the faults of wordiness and abstraction that have been the theme of earlier chapters. It is not just that they are long and require boiling down. There is more to this business than that. The stories do waste space but they are also duller than they need to be. As well as boiling down they need spicing with a sense that they are about people. Quick editing could have revived these stories; rewriting could have rescued them. Neither need involve losing a single fact. The way this might have been achieved by applying the text-editing principles already set will be demonstrated in this chapter. But it will be more effective if it involves you, the reader in the way described below.

Editing Copy or Rewriting

When all or some of the faults so far discussed appear in copy, the deskman has three basic choices.

• Edit on copy—this means accepting the structure of the story but improving it by detailed work on the words. This is the quickest method.

• Rewrite entirely—the slowest method but unavoidable in bad cases.

● Mix both techniques—rewrite the lead into the story but edit the rest of it on copy. There are all sorts of gradations in this. The most straightforward is to write off a new lead paragraph on a separate folio, and then pick up the rest of the copy for editing as it is.

Or you can move nearer to a full-scale rewrite. This happens when the key human fact is buried in the story and not in the intro at all. Select the most interesting or important sentences or paragraphs, rewrite them as a lead, on separate folios or on copy. Next rewrite another sentence or two to make the new lead link with the existing copy. Finally, when the link is established edit the rest of the story on copy. When you come to the point you transposed to the first sentence you delete it in its old position, of course, and make sure the story still flows over the gap. (In this operation you will also take care to renumber the folios.)

In the following examples (Exercises 1–5), version *A* is the story as it appeared in print. Version *B* is how that same report could have been improved by quickly editing it on copy without deleting essential facts. Version *C* is how the story could have been rewritten, given, say, fifteen minutes beyond the time available for straight editing on copy. In rewriting, of course, time always has to be allowed over and above that needed to think and write the words down. The words have then to be checked against the original for accuracy in every detail. Rewriting is a waste of time if it introduces error.

A good exercise with each story that follows is to type out version *A* in double spacing. Then rough-edit it on copy yourself before examining my edited versions to compare changes and space saved.

Next, having studied the *B* versions, rewrite the story completely and compare that with the rewritten *C* version in this book. I do not pretend that these are the last word in text editing. Version *B* must be done quickly—not more than fifteen minutes on any of these stories. Version *C* may take up to half an hour.

Exercise One

Version A

ROAD TOLL STARTS CLIMB

by the Associated Press

The toll of traffic deaths among Americans celebrating the nation's freedom rose steadily yesterday.

The count climbed to 110 for the Independence Day holiday period that began at 6 p.m. Wednesday and will end at midnight Sunday.

The National Safety Council commented that, while the number was pushing up, it was not keeping pace with the total for the corresponding time of the four-day Fourth of July observance in 1961 when it reached a record 509.

The worst single accident cost the lives of six members of a family from Butler, Pa., who had set out for a pleasure ride in their new car.

Dry, pleasant weather in most sections of the country encouraged heavy travel.

The council has estimated that motor vehicle accidents may kill 550 to 650 persons during the four-day Independence observance.

That would be a record far exceeding the hold mark for a July 4th period of 509 set in 1961.

The record for a holiday period of any kind was established during a four-day observance of Christmas in 1956. It is 706.

To draw comparisons, the Associated Press made a survey of traffic fatalities during the four-day non-holiday period running from 6 p.m. Wednesday, June 19, to midnight Sunday, June 23. The tally was 458.

Traffic deaths, holding at record levels, have averaged 100 a day through the first five months of this year.

July 4 boating accidents cost 12 lives and drownings 40.

Note how the human interest has been diluted by abstractions like 'road toll'. But buried in here is the highly newsworthy human story of a whole family being killed. It is a specific human detail that brings the abstract 'road toll' home to readers. Note how much extra verbiage and repetition appear, saying in ten words what can be said more comprehensibly in two. It sounds like official language untouched by human hand. More detail should have been given of the family tragedy. The story cries out for this awareness that *people* are involved.

Version B

~~The toll of~~ Traffic deaths among Americans celebrating the nation's freedom rose steadily yesterday.

The ~~count climbed to~~ *total is* 110 for the Independence Day holiday *period* that began at 6 p.m. Wednesday and will end at midnight Sunday. *But,*

The National Safety Council ~~commented that,~~ *says this* ~~while the number was pushing up, it was not keeping pace with the total for~~ *is lower than* the corresponding time ~~of the four-day Fourth of July observance~~ in 1961 when ~~it reached~~ a record 509 */ died.*

The worst single accident ~~cost the lives of~~ *yesterday killed* six ~~members~~ of a family from Butler, Pa., who had set out for ~~a~~ pleasure ~~ride~~ in their new car.

Dry, pleasant weather in most ~~sections of the country~~ *parts* encouraged heavy travel.

The council has estimated that ~~motor vehicle~~ *car* accidents may kill 550 to 650 ~~persons during the~~ *this* four-day ~~Independence observance~~ *holiday.*

That would be a record ~~far exceeding the hold~~ *well over the old* ~~mark for a July 4th period~~ *one* of 509 ~~set~~ in 1961.

The record for ~~a~~ *any* holiday ~~period of any kind~~ *is 706 killed*

~~was established during~~ *over* a four-/days ~~observance of~~ *at*
Christmas ~~is~~ 1956. ~~It is 706.~~

~~To draw~~ [*For* comparison,/ the Associated Press ~~made~~
~~a survey of~~ *surveyed* traffic ~~fatalities during~~ *deaths over* the four-day
non-holiday period ~~running~~ from 6 p.m. Wednesday,
June 19, to midnight Sunday, June 23. The tally
was 458.

[Traffic deaths, holding at record levels, have
averaged 100 a day ~~through~~ *in* the first five months of
this year.

[July 4 boating accidents cost 12 lives and
drownings 40.

Version C

[Version *A* typeset for comparison]

FAMILY OF SIX DIES
Road Toll at 110

ROAD TOLL STARTS CLIMB
by the Associated Press

(AP) Six of a family from Butler, Pa., out for pleasure in their new car, died yesterday in the worst accident so far of the Independence Day holidays.

The toll among Americans celebrating the nation's freedom rose steadily as dry pleasant weather encouraged heavy travel in most parts. By last night 110 had died since 6 p.m. on Wednesday.

The National Safety Council said, however, deaths were not keeping pace with last year. It had previously estimated that 550 to 650 might die between Wednesday and the end of the holiday on Sunday, which would top the Independence record of 509 deaths in 1961. The all-time record for holiday deaths is 706 over four days at Christmas, 1956.

The toll of traffic deaths among Americans celebrating the nation's freedom rose steadily yesterday.

The count climbed to 110 for the Independence Day holiday period that began at 6 p.m. Wednesday and will end at midnight Sunday.

The National Safety Council commented that, while the number was pushing up, it was not keeping pace with the total for the corresponding time of the four-day Fourth of July observance in 1961 when it reached a record 509.

The worst single accident cost the lives of six members of a family from Butler, Pa., who had set out for a pleasure ride in their new car.

Dry, pleasant weather in most sections of the country encouraged heavy travel.

The council has estimated that motor vehicle accidents may kill 550 to 650 persons during the four-day Independence observance.

That would be a record far exceeding the hold mark for a July 4th period of 509 set in 1961.

The record for a holiday period of any kind was established during a four-day observance of Christmas in 1956. It is 706.

To draw comparisons, the Associated Press made a survey of traffic fatalities during the four-day non-holiday period running from 6 p.m. Wednesday, June 19, to midnight Sunday, June 23. The tally was 458.

Traffic deaths, holding at record levels, have averaged 100 a day through the first five months of this year.

July 4 boating accidents cost 12 lives and drownings 40.

Exercise Two

Version A

The shape of Britain's Navy of the future, contained within an absolute budget ceiling of just over £30 million, and even as low as £25 million, for any one ship, will be outlined in a Government White Paper on defence to be published, I understand, before Parliament rises for the summer recess.

Inevitably, the White Paper will reveal substantial cutting-back, restricting the future Fleet to ships of medium tonnage, and ruling out the possibility of a mini-carrier, for which many naval 'die-hards' have fought. Instead the accent will be on the provision of strong helicopter potential for all future ships, and on anti-submarine warfare improvements.

It is probable, too, that the White Paper will contain at least an outline for the development of missile capacity in almost all future vessels, and a breakaway from the absurdly expensive provision of ships of the Type 82 Class of guided missile 'cruiser'. The continuation of the present programme of nuclear-powered hunter-killer submarines is assured.

Future policy for the Navy will, I understand, be closely related to the probable requirements of both the Army and the RAF. The White Paper will outline a strong development in the amphibious field, stringently tailored to the Government's pronouncements on co-operation with independent countries in what is loosely described as a brush-fire war situation.

The decision not to build a mini-carrier has been influenced by doubts on the practicability of carriers in numbers smaller than the vast American strength. It is felt that any carrier arm numbering fewer than six ships is unlikely, after the mid-seventies, to prove viable even against second league powers, which have been equipped by the super-powers. Air co-operation will be provided necessarily, therefore, by other means.

Helicopter development will substantially enhance the anti-submarine warfare performance of the Fleet, and in most circumstances will provide at least limited reconnaissance capacity. It could clearly be extended in the future towards providing an answer to the development of small missile gunboats rapidly being extended by, for example, Russia.

The programme as a whole will be less than the optimists hoped for, but larger than the pessimists feared.   Cuts, to fall in line with Britain's financial situation, will apply to all three Services, but again it is now believed that they will be less crippling than had once been feared.

   Delay and obscurity as to the Government's intentions since the tabling of the annual White Paper in February have markedly affected service attitudes, and the need for a positive statement of intention is now considered urgent.   The White Paper has, in fact, been drafted.

There are too many administrative abstractions in the intro and not enough specifics—battleships, cruisers and helicopters. A 'budget ceiling' is harder to imagine than a battleship. The rest of the copy is full of wasted words. Type out this story before going further and try your own editing on it before looking at my version *B*.

   Did you save by attacking the wasteful phrases—the provision of, it is probable, development of missile capacity, a strong development in the amphibious field (the amphibious *field* indeed!), brush-fire war situation, financial situation, etc.?

Version B

~~The shape of~~ Britain's Navy of the future,
contained within ~~an absolute budget~~ *a* ceiling of
~~just over~~ £30 million~~, and even as low as £25
million~~ for any one ship, will be outlined in
a Government White Paper ~~on defence~~ to be
published, I understand, before Parliament rises
for ~~the~~ summer~~, recess~~.

~~Inevitably,~~ The White Paper will reveal
substantial ~~cutting back,~~ *cuts,* restricting the future
Fleet to ships of medium tonnage, and ruling out
the possibility of a mini-carrier, for which ~~many~~
naval 'die-hards' have fought. Instead the accent
will be on ~~the provision of strong~~ helicopter*s*
~~potential~~ for all future ships, and on anti-
submarine warfare improvements.

~~It is probable, too, that~~ The White Paper will
~~contain at least an~~ *probably* outline ~~for the~~ *missile* development ~~of
missile capacity~~ in almost all future vessels, and
a breakaway from *providing* the absurdly expensive ~~provision
of ships of the~~ Type 82 Class of guided missile
'cruiser'. The ~~continuation of the present~~ programme
of nuclear-powered hunter-killer submarines ~~is assured~~ *will go on.*

[Naval

~~Future~~ policy ~~for the Navy~~ will, I understand, be closely related to the probable ~~requirements~~ *need* of both ~~the~~ Army and ~~the~~ RAF. ~~The White Paper~~ will *There will be* outline ~~a strong development in the~~ *money for* amphibious *equipment,* ~~field,~~ stringently tailored to the Government's *desire to* ~~pronouncements on~~ co-operati~~on~~ *e* with independent countries in ~~what is loosely described as a~~ brush-fire war~~s situation~~.

The decision not to build a mini-carrier has been influenced by doubts on the practicability of carriers in numbers smaller than the vast American strength. It is felt that any carrier arm numbering fewer than six ships is unlikely, after the mid-seventies, to prove viable even against second league powers, which have been equipped by the super-powers. Air *support* ~~co-operation~~ will be provided ~~necessarily, therefore,~~ by other means.

Helicopter~~s development~~ will substantially enhance the anti-submarine warfare *capability* ~~performance~~ of the Fleet, and in most circumstances will provide at least limited reconnaissance capacity. *More helicopters* ~~It could clearly be extended~~ *could cope with* ~~in the future towards providing an answer to~~ the development of small missile gunboats rapidly being extended by, for example, Russia.

The programme as a whole will be less than the optimists hoped for, but larger than the pessimists feared. Cuts ~~to fall in line with Britain's financial situation~~ will apply to all three Services, ~~but again it is now believed that they will be less crippling than had once been feared.~~

~~Delay and~~ Obscurity *about* ~~as to~~ the Government's intentions since the tabling of the annual White Paper in February *has* ~~have~~ markedly affected service attitudes, and the need for a positive statement of intention is now considered urgent. The White Paper has, in fact, been drafted.

Version C

Britain's new economy Navy—within a budget of £30m—will be restricted to medium-tonnage ships, but will have a strong force of helicopters, more anti-submarine weapons, and amphibious equipment.

These plans will be outlined in a Government White Paper, I understand, before Parliament rises for summer. The programme will be less than the optimists hoped for but larger than the pessimists feared. There will be no mini-carrier, for which many naval diehards fought, but it is probable the White Paper will contain at least an outline for the development of missiles in almost all future ships. There will be a breakaway from providing the absurdly costly ships of the Type 82 Class of guided missile 'cruiser'. The programme of nuclear-powered hunter-killer submarines will go on.

The mini-carrier decision has been influenced by doubts on the effectiveness of carriers in numbers smaller than the vast American strength. It is felt that any carrier arm numbering fewer than six ships is unlikely after the mid-70s to be a match against even second-league powers which have been equipped by the super-powers.

Air co-operation will be provided by other methods. Helicopters will be part of the anti-submarine force and will help with reconnaissance. They may help to meet the threat of small missile gunboats rapidly being extended by, for example, Russia.

[Version A typeset for comparison]

The shape of Britain's Navy of the future, contained within an absolute budget ceiling of just over £30 million, and even as low as £25 million, for any one ship, will be outlined in a Government White Paper on defence to be published, I understand, before Parliament rises for the summer recess.

Inevitably, the White Paper will reveal substantial cutting-back, restricting the future Fleet to ships of medium tonnage, and ruling out the possibility of a mini-carrier, for which many naval 'die-hards' have fought. Instead the accent will be on the provision of strong helicopter potential for all future ships, and on anti-submarine warfare improvements.

It is probable, too, that the White Paper will contain at least an outline for the development of missile capacity in almost all future vessels, and a breakaway from the absurdly expensive provision of ships of the Type 82 Class of guided missile 'cruiser'. The continuation of the present programme of nuclear-powered hunter-killer submarines is assured.

Future policy for the Navy will, I understand, be closely related to the probable requirements of both the Army and the RAF. The White Paper will outline a strong development in the amphibious field, stringently tailored to the Government's pronouncements on co-operation with independent countries in what is loosely described as a brush-fire war situation.

The decision not to build a mini-carrier has been influenced by doubts on the practicability of carriers in numbers smaller than the vast American strength. It is felt that any carrier arm numbering fewer than six ships is unlikely, after the mid-seventies, to prove viable even against second league powers, which have been equipped by the super-powers. Air co-operation will be provided necessarily, therefore, by other means.

Helicopter development will substantially enhance the anti-submarine warfare performance of the Fleet, and in most circumstances will provide at least limited reconnaissance capacity. It could clearly be extended in the future towards providing an answer to the development of small missile gunboats rapidly being extended by, for example, Russia.

The programme as a whole will be less than the optimists hoped for, but larger than the pessimists feared. Cuts, to fall in line with Britain's financial situation, will apply to all three Services, but again it is now believed that they will be less crippling than had once been feared.

Delay and obscurity as to the Government's intentions since the tabling of the annual White Paper in February have markedly affected service attitudes, and the need for a positive statement of intention is now considered urgent. The White Paper has, in fact, been drafted.

Exercise Three

Version A

Twenty-eight tremors have been recorded here following yesterday's earthquake which burst a reservoir about 60 miles north-east of Santiago and buried the village of El Cobre in a sea of mud, the Seismological Institute said today.

Officials said 27 bodies had been recovered from El Cobre and another 121 people were missing out of the 400 inhabitants of the village which was hit by a 1,000 yard wide sea of mud and rock. Other reports put the total toll of the earthquake as high as 600.

The headline given to this story—version *A*—naturally caught one's eye: SEA OF MUD ENGULFED CHILE VILLAGE (and how much better if the deskman had written ENGULFS). But look at the frustrations the reader has to endure when his eye skips to the story—38 words of intro and a long second par with the people at the end. Version *B* is the quickest way to edit this story *and* bring something about people near the top. But better still is to let the tremors take second place to the victims of the disaster.

Version B

JEL COBRE, a village of 400, was buried
~~Twenty-eight tremors have been recorded here~~
in a 1,000-yard sea of mud after an
~~following yesterday's~~ earthquake ~~which~~ burst a

reservoir about 60 miles north-east of Santiago,
~~and buried the village of El Cobre in a sea of mud,~~ yesterday.

~~the Seismological Institute said today.~~

[Officials said 27 bodies had been recovered

~~from El Cobre~~ and another 121 ~~people~~ were missing,

~~out of the 400 inhabitants of the village which was~~

~~hit by a 1,000-yard-wide sea of mud and rock.~~ Other

reports put the total toll of the earthquake as high

as 600.

[The Seismological Institute reported
a further 28 tremors yesterday.

Version C

Nearly 150 of the 400 inhabitants of the village of El Cobre, 60 miles north-east of Santiago, are feared dead, buried beneath a sea of mud and rock produced by an earthquake yesterday.

The violent earthquake—28 tremors were recorded yesterday—burst a reservoir and produced a 1,000 yard wide avalanche of mud and rock. Twenty-seven bodies have been recovered and another 121 people are missing.

[Version A typeset for comparison]

Twenty-eight tremors have been recorded here following yesterday's earthquake which burst a reservoir about 60 miles north-east of Santiago and buried the village of El Cobre in a sea of mud, the Seismological Institute said today.

Officials said 27 bodies had been recovered from El Cobre and another 121 people were missing out of the 400 inhabitants of the village which was hit by a 1,000 yard wide sea of mud and rock. Other reports put the total toll of the earthquake as high as 600.

Exercise Four

Version A

Uncertainty about mortgage rates has, in the last three months, limited the marked home-ownership advance of recent years, according to the National Federation of Building Trades Employers.

A survey just completed shows that private house-purchase figures have fallen away sharply compared with three months ago.

Despite the improvement in the availability of mortgages, the number of empty houses awaiting buyers is rising. A spokesman for the Federation yesterday blamed the situation on the Government's failure to say when, if and by how much, interest rates will be reduced.

Version B

Uncertainty about mortgage rates has, in the
last three months, ~~limited the marked~~ *checked the* home-ownership advance of recent years, ~~according to~~ *says* the
National Federation of Building Trades Employers.

~~A survey just completed shows that private~~
~~house-purchase figures have fallen away sharply~~
~~compared with three months ago.~~

Despite ~~the improvement in the availability~~ *easier access to*
~~of~~ mortgages, the number of empty houses awaiting
buyers is rising. A spokesman ~~for the~~ Federation
yesterday blamed ~~the situation~~ *this* on the Government's
failure to say when, if and by how much, interest
rates will be reduced.

Version C

[Version *A* typeset for comparison]

Fewer people are buying houses—because of uncertainty about mortgage rates, says the National Federation of Building Trades Employers.

It is easier to get mortgages, but a Federation survey reveals more empty houses and fewer private purchases in the last three months. A federation spokesman yesterday blamed the Government, for failing to say when, if and by how much interest rates will be cut.

Uncertainty about mortgage rates has, in the last three months, limited the marked home-ownership advance of recent years, according to the National Federation of Building Trades Employers.

A survey just completed shows that private house-purchase figures have fallen away sharply compared with three months ago.

Despite the improvement in the availability of mortgages, the number of empty houses awaiting buyers is rising. A spokesman for the Federation yesterday blamed the situation on the Government's failure to say when, if and by how much, interest rates will be reduced.

Exercise Five

Version A

New York (AP) – Tuberculosis, thought to be near extinction a few years ago, has had an alarming resurgence in New York City this year, reports City Health Commissioner Dr George James.

In discussing the comeback of the disease yesterday, James said the number of TB cases increased 12 per cent in the first eight months of this year. He estimated there would be 5,000 new cases this year, about the same number as in 1959.

'What is especially alarming', James told newsmen, 'is that a trend has been reversed.'

Most of the new cases, he said, were among Negroes and Puerto Ricans. He noted that slum conditions represent 'a greater opportunity for infection'.

In Albany yesterday, a spokesman for the State Health Department said the TB increase in New York City 'may portend' a similar rise in urban areas upstate.

However, the first six months of 1963 show fewer cases outside New York City than in 1962. In 1962 there were 1,080 cases reported from January to June. From January through June this year the count was 852 cases.

It is extraordinary how easily a report about people is dehumanised. Here is an agency report, as published in a daily newspaper, which is about tuberculosis and which goes almost to any lengths to avoid conceding that 'TB cases' are people. Note how the report says 'many new cases were among Negroes and Puerto Ricans' when it means many of the victims *were* Negroes and Puerto Ricans. Note also 'slum conditions' and 'overcrowded conditions'. Note again how confusingly figures are presented.

Version B

New York (AP) — Tuberculosis, thought to be near extinction a few years ago, has had an alarming resurgence in New York City this year, reports City Health Commissioner Dr George James.

~~In discussing the comeback of the disease yesterday, James said the number of~~ TB ~~cases~~ *had* increased 12 per cent in the first eight months of this year, *and* He estimated there would be 5,000 new ~~cases~~ *victims* this year. *This is* about the same number as in 1959, *but James told newsmen:* 'What is especially alarming ~~, James told newsmen~~, is that a trend has been reversed.'

Most of the new ~~cases~~ *sufferers,* he said, were ~~among~~ Negroes and Puerto Ricans. ~~He noted that~~ Slum ~~conditions~~ represent*ed* 'a greater opportunity for infection'.

In Albany yesterday, a ~~spokesman for the~~ State Health Department *spokesman* said the ~~TB~~ increase in New York City 'may portend' a ~~similar~~ rise in urban areas upstate.

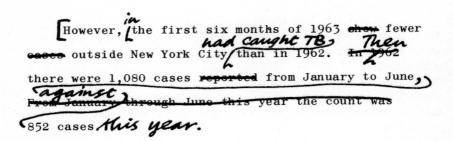

However, [in the first six months of 1963 ~~show~~ fewer ~~cases~~ outside New York City had caught TB, than in 1962. ~~In 1962~~ Then there were 1,080 cases ~~reported~~ from January to June, against ~~From January through June this year the count was~~ 852 cases this year.

Version C

More people in New York City are catching tuberculosis this year.

City Health Commissioner Dr George James says that TB, thought to be nearly extinct, has claimed 12 per cent more victims than last year in the first eight months. He estimates about 5,000 will get TB this year.

This is about the same as 1959, but James said it was 'especially alarming' that the trend has been reversed.

Most of the new victims are Negroes and Puerto Ricans. Slums and overcrowded homes presented 'a greater opportunity for infection'.

In Albany yesterday a State Health Department spokesman said New York City's TB increase 'may portend' a similar rise in urban areas upstate. However, in the first six months of 1963 outside New York City fewer people than in 1962 had caught TB—852 this year against 1,080 in 1962.

[Version *A* typeset for comparison]

New York (AP)—Tuberculosis, thought to be near extinction a few years ago, has had an alarming resurgence in New York City this year, reports City Health Commissioner Dr George James.

In discussing the comeback of the disease yesterday, James said the number of TB cases increased 12 per cent in the first eight months of this year. He estimated there would be 5,000 new cases this year, about the same number as in 1959.

'What is especially alarming', James told newsmen, 'is that a trend has been reversed.'

Most of the new cases, he said, were among Negroes and Puerto Ricans. He noted that slum conditions represent 'a greater opportunity for infection'.

In Albany yesterday, a spokesman for the State Health Department said the TB increase in New York City 'may portend' a similar rise in urban areas upstate.

However, the first six months of 1963 show fewer cases outside New York City than in 1962. In 1962 there were 1,080 cases reported from January to June. From January through June this year the count was 852 cases.

Exercise Six

The text editor who has got so far can conclude by testing himself against a possible future rival—the editing computer. (But take heart: every editorial computer will have to be programmed by someone with editorial skills.) What follows are experimental examples of a remarkable computer program, called ANPAT, developed by the Research Centre of the American Newspaper Publishers Association.

Without human intervention, a computer using the ANPAT programme takes an original wire service TTS tape story (version *A*) and reduces it to any length requested.

It responds to instructions to produce a story which will make so many lines of type. Generally it is within three lines of the requested length; occasionally it misses, on the experimental examples, by six or seven lines. The human text editor should first imagine he is handling the same story as metal or film after setting, and make cuts which reduce the story to the number of lines requested without resetting. He will, like the ANPAT program, need a clear idea of what is bone and what is flesh in the structure of the story. The ANPAT reductions (versions *B* and *C* here) are by deletion of subsidiary material paragraph by paragraph. This undoubtedly the quickest way, though the human text editor could also make quick cuts in metal by deleting superfluous words at the end of a paragraph, especially where they make 'widows' (short lines of type). In this way he will—as is often required in editing on the stone—reduce a story precisely to the number of lines requested.

There is a second exercise which only the human text editor can do and at which the computer of the human brain, once trained, will probably always be able to beat the electronic computer. This is to regard the original story at version *A* not as metal or film but as raw copy. It can be edited by the word. That exercise should reveal something else: the opportunity for close editing and story improvement sacrificed by those newspapers which feed into typecasting machines agency tape unedited by the host newspaper. Untouched, one might say, by human mind.

Version A

ORIGINAL 89 LINES

Geneva (AP) Britain called on the world's advanced powers Tuesday to draft a new treaty banning the production and use of bacteriological weapons.

Outlines of convention to outlaw germ warfare were presented to the 17-nation disarmament conference by British Minister of State Fred Mulley.

But the Soviet Union was hostile and the United States was reported cool to the British proposal.

The convention would first have to be approved by 'a list of states— say 10–12—considered by an appropriate international body to be those most advanced in microbiological research work,' Mulley said.

It would come into force after ratification by these nations 'plus a suitably large number of other states.'

Mulley argued that the 1925 Geneva Convention banning the use of chemical and bacteriological weapons is now obsolete. Many nations, including the United States, have not ratified it. And others who do adhere to it, including Britain, reserve the right to use such weapons against nonsigners of the convention.

The Geneva protocol also only bans the use, but not the manufacture, of bacteriological weapons, and it does not take into account the latest scientific developments in the field of microbiology, Mulley said.

After getting wind of the British proposal, the chief Soviet delegate, Alexei A. Roschin, recently said the Geneva protocol is sufficient. He argued it prevented the use of germ and chemical warfare during World War II.

Mulley retorted that Adolf Hitler was not restrained by the Geneva protocol, but by the fear of retaliation adding: 'Respect for international law was not one of his strongest points as far as I recall.'

The United States is reliably reported to have tried to persuade the British to shelve the plan.

This is because the United States and the Soviet Union have been making progress on nuclear disarmament. Following the treaty to halt the spread of nuclear weapons, both sides have agreed to talk about limiting defensive and offensive ballistic missile systems.

They also are largely in agreement on a Soviet proposal for a treaty banning the installation of nuclear devices on the ocean floor. The United States is believed to feel the British initiative could jeopardize nuclear agreements.

If Britain can get enough support from the nonaligned nations, the two superpowers may be forced to go along on the germ warfare treaty.

The international convention proposed by Britain would eliminate stockpiles of bacteriological material for hostile purposes, ban research into such weapons, and provide neutral international investigations on the soil of any signatory state suspected of violating the treaty. This last is enough to arouse Soviet hostility. The Russians refused to go along on any kind of inspection.

The British proposal would call for U.N. Security Council action against any nonsignatory state threatening the convention.

Version B

75 LINES REQUESTED
76 LINES RECEIVED

Geneva (AP) Britain called on the world's advanced powers Tuesday to draft a new treaty banning the production and use of bacteriological weapons.

Outlines of convention to outlaw germ warfare were presented to the 17-nation disarmament conference by British Minister of State Fred Mulley.

But the Soviet Union was hostile and the United States was reported cool to the British proposal.

The convention would first have to be approved by 'a list of states—say 10–12—considered by an appropriate international body to be those most advanced in microbiological research work,' Mulley said.

Mulley argued that the 1925 Geneva Convention banning the use of chemical and bacteriological weapons is now obsolete. Many nations, including the United States, have not ratified it. And others who do adhere to it, including Britain, reserve the right to use such weapons against nonsigners of the convention.

The Geneva protocol also only bans the use, but not the manufacture, of bacteriological weapons, and it does not take into account the latest scientific developments in the field of microbiology, Mulley said.

After getting wind of the British proposal, the chief Soviet delegate, Alexei A. Roschin, recently said the Geneva protocol is sufficient. He argued it prevented the use of germ and chemical warfare during World War II.

The United States is reliably reported to have tried to persuade the British to shelve the plan.

This is because the United States and the Soviet Union have been making progress on nuclear disarmament. Following the treaty to halt the spread of nuclear weapons, both sides have agreed to talk about limiting defensive and offensive ballistic missile systems.

They also are largely in agreement on a Soviet proposal for a treaty banning the installation of nuclear devices on the ocean floor. The United States is believed to feel the British initiative could jeopardize nuclear agreements.

The international convention proposed by Britain would eliminate stockpiles of bacteriological material for hostile purposes, ban research into such weapons, and provide neutral international investigations on the soil of any signatory state suspected of violating the treaty. This last is enough to arouse Soviet hostility. The Russians refused to go along on any kind of inspection.

The British proposal would call for U.N. Security Council action against any nonsignatory state threatening the convention.

- - - - - - ANPAT - - - - - -

Version C

33 LINES REQUESTED
32 LINES RECEIVED

Geneva (AP) Britain called on the world's advanced powers Tuesday to draft a new treaty banning the production and use of bacteriological weapons.

Outlines of convention to outlaw germ warfare were presented to the 17-nation disarmament conference by British Minister of State Fred Mulley.

Mulley argued that the 1925 Geneva Convention banning the use of chemical and bacteriological weapons is now obsolete. Many nations, including the United States, have not ratified it. And others who do adhere to it, including Britain, reserve the right to use such weapons against nonsigners of the convention.

The international convention proposed by Britain would eliminate stockpiles of bacteriological material for hostile purposes, ban research into such weapons, and provide neutral international investigations on the soil of any signatory state suspected of violating the treaty. This last is enough to arouse Soviet hostility. The Russians refused to go along on any kind of inspection.

- - - - - - ANPAT - - - - - -

Bibliography

English and Text

BERNSTEIN, Theodore M, and GARST, Robert E. *Headlines and Deadlines*. New York: Columbia University Press, 1961.
Manual for the copy editor by managing editors of the *New York Times*. Does not discuss typography or graphic design, and is drawn entirely from American practices, but is excellent on detailed text editing.

BERNSTEIN, Theodore M. *Watch Your Language*. New York: Channel Press, 1958.
Pungent guide to good newspaper English by a former managing editor of the *New York Times*.

BERNSTEIN, Theodore M. *More Language that Needs Watching*. New York: Channel Press, 1962.

BREWSTER, William T. *Writing English Prose*. New York: Henry Holt and Co, 1913.
Old but still valuable criticism.

FLESCH, Rudolf. *The Art of Readable Writing*. New York: Harper and Bros, 1949.
Usefully attempts to formulate detailed rules for clear expression, some of which will help deskmen.

GOWERS, Sir Ernest. *Plain Words*. London: Her Majesty's Stationery Office, 1948.
Masterly analysis of confused official English.

GRAVES, Robert, and HODGE, Alan. *The Reader Over Your Shoulder*. London: Jonathan Cape, 1948.
Principles for clear expressive English eloquently argued with many examples. Particularly good on official English.

HARRIS, Geoffrey, and SPARK, David. *Practical Newspaper Reporting*. London: Heinemann, 1966.
Closely written textbook for English newspaper reporters, but with some valuable thoughts for text editors. Packed with sound advice.

JORDAN, Lewis (ed.). *The New York Times Style Book for Editors and Writers*. New York: McGraw Hill, 1962.
Alphabetical style book emphasising precision in writing.

MENCKEN, H L. *The American Language. Supplement One*. New York: Alfred A Knopf, 1945.

NELSON, Harold L, and TEETER, Dwight L. *Law of Mass Communications*. Mineola, New York: Foundation Press, 1969.
This and Phelps and Hamilton's book are recommended for the American deskman; with prudence they can be consulted by deskmen in all English-speaking countries.

PARTRIDGE, Eric. *The Concise Usage and Abusage*. London: Hamish Hamilton, 1954.
Takes up where Fowler left off.

PHELPS, Bob, and HAMILTON, Douglas. *Libel: A Guide to Rights, Risks and Responsibilities*. New York: Macmillan; revised and published in Collier Books paperback, 1969. *See* Nelson and Teeter.

POTTER, Simeon. *Our Language*. Harmondsworth: Pelican, 1964.
Useful chapters on the sentence, authority and usage, slang and dialect, and British and American English.

SELLERS, Leslie. *The Simple Subs Book*. Oxford: Pergamon Press, 1968.
Brief but witty basic book for English sub-editors by production editor of the London *Daily Mail*.

SELLERS, Leslie. *Doing it in Style*. Oxford: Pergamon Press, 1968.
Alphabetical style-book aimed to be of practical value to the deskman. Aimed strictly at English sub-editors.

Index

Editing and Design

A Five-volume Manual of English, Typography and Layout

Harold Evans's major work also includes:

BOOK TWO: HANDLING NEWSPAPER TEXT

The practical business of marking up copy for the printer is explained and there are examples to work through. The typography of text setting is examined with new insight and the book shows how a big running news story was handled for publication through all six editions of a morning newspaper. Copious typographical examples.

BOOK THREE: NEWS HEADLINES

Here the techniques and skills of headline writing are related to real news stories. The book shows what typefaces and treatment to use and includes a headline vocabulary—a deskman's thesaurus of words to give the right simplicity and punch. Many typographical examples and exercises.

BOOK FOUR: PICTURE EDITING

The book tells how picture selection and creative cropping can achieve maximum effect. All the practical knowledge needed in handling pictures is given, including the techniques of picture-sequence and the neglected area of graphics. With many outstanding illustrations and comparisons of treatment.

BOOK FIVE: NEWSPAPER DESIGN

Harold Evans shows that newspapers can be designed to communicate, superseding the messy legacies of printing tradition. Detailed instruction covers such things as the individual page, pages as spreads, giving sub-sections their own identity, relating advertising and editorial content; it demonstrates that regularity of format can be achieved without sacrificing flexibility. There is, in addition, a comparative analysis of design merits and defects of newspapers from all over the world. Extensively illustrated with photographs and typographical examples.